Raising Our Voices,
Breaking the Chain

RAISING OUR VOICES, BREAKING THE CHAIN

THE IMPERIAL HOTEL OCCUPATION AS PROPHETIC POLITICS

Terry Easton

For James & Ann,
Thanks for all your support!
Best wishes,
Terry

The Open Door Community Press
Atlanta

To purchase additional copies of
Raising Our Voices, Breaking the Chain,
phone, e-mail, or send an order in writing to:

The Open Door Community
910 Ponce de Leon Avenue N.E.
Atlanta GA 30306
(404) 874-9652
opendoorcomm@bellsouth.net

Cover and text layout and design by Barbara Segal
Copy edited by Julie Martin
Author photo by Annie Gannon Kaufman
Michael Vosburg-Casey photo by Calvin Kimbrough

*The Lord has told us what is good. What he requires of us is this:
to do what is just, to show constant love, and to live in
humble fellowship with our God.*
Micah 6:8

*Justice is never forged by people who sit and quietly enjoy dreams of peace
and harmony. Justice is forged when people join hands to work together with
love in their hearts and fire in their bones. It is forged when people respond to
particular concrete expressions of oppression and say, "No. No more."*
Murphy Davis

Dedication

This book is dedicated to the courageous, though largely invisible
and voiceless, homeless people who occupied the abandoned
Imperial Hotel in Atlanta, Georgia, for sixteen
days in June 1990.

In Memory

Michael Vosburg-Casey, 1974 – 2013

A gentle, courageous soul whose life remains as an inspiration
to action for all who love justice, peace, and the radical
vision of the Beloved Community.

Contents

PROLOGUE
A BATTLE ON PEACHTREE STREET

In the early morning hours of June 18, 1990, a storm was brewing on Peachtree Street, Atlanta's north-south corridor, the core from which the city's power and commerce radiated. This was no ordinary storm. In fact, the weather was typical for early summer in Atlanta: warm and humid. This was a storm that involved people, not weather. In the four o'clock darkness, eight activists committed a courageous act that rattled Atlanta's power structure: they broke into the abandoned Imperial Hotel — an eight-story, early twentieth-century structure that, in its heyday, housed middle-class tourists and business travelers. Empty and in severe disrepair amid the shiny modern towers nearby, the Imperial symbolized Atlanta's past while the new towers represented its future. On another level, one more aligned with the activists' concern as the number of homeless people in Atlanta increased, the empty Imperial symbolized the failure of the city to provide ample affordable housing for its residents.

The Imperial Hotel in Atlanta, 1990. Photo courtesy of the Open Door Community.

With a commitment to taking their Christian and civil rights era-inspired beliefs to the streets to disrupt "business as usual," the activists, known collectively as People for Urban Justice (PUJ), broke into the abandoned Imperial Hotel at 4:00 a.m. and unfurled a banner from the top floor windows with the message "House the Homeless Here!" The sign and the accompanying demonstration on the streets below were designed to bring media attention to the city's dearth of affordable housing. PUJ members expected to be removed and arrested in short order, but police, city officials, and the hotel's owner, architect and developer John Portman, did not remove or arrest them. So PUJ decided to remain in the hotel until their demands for affordable housing were met or until they were forcibly removed. Meanwhile, they opened the hotel to homeless people, and they all stayed through the night. That one night became the sixteen nights of the occupation of the Imperial Hotel.

The occupation and its aftermath exposed Atlanta's landscape of power while illuminating three visions of the city. Theologian and scholar-activist Peter Gathje dramatically characterizes these visions: "On the one side are those who see the city in light of the Beloved Community – an inclusive, welcoming, more egalitarian, democratic, communal vision. On another side are those who see the city in light of Empire – a hierarchical, elitist, bureaucratic plutocracy in which the economically and politically powerful reign, sometimes with a 'noblesse oblige' but always with a command over others. And then there are those moving between those visions, trying to negotiate between them."[1]

In the struggle for affordable housing on Peachtree Street and beyond, individuals and groups emerged that sharpened the contours of these visions. PUJ and its supporters represented the Beloved Community. Central Atlanta Progress and the city's ruling elite represented Empire. Progressive housing developers saw a crevice that opened during the occupation, a space they hoped to fill with affordable housing.

Who won the battle on Peachtree Street? Which vision prevailed? If you have spent any time in Atlanta, the answers to these questions may seem obvious. But keep reading; in doing so, you will discover a story about Atlanta and its people that will surprise and inspire you.

METHODS

This book tells the story of the Imperial Hotel occupation from the perspective of activists affiliated with the Open Door Community. This history is based largely on oral accounts of what happened more than twenty-five years ago. I present the history as accurately as possible and, at times, have "triangulated" sources – checked with multiple interviewees or archival sources – to verify what happened on a particular day or during a specific event.

The people interviewed for this book are generally those who were connected to the action that took place either before, during, or after the occupation.[2] I interviewed five of the eight initial activists who entered the hotel June 18. The other three have passed away.

Historian Todd Moye's comments are helpful in making sense of the complex relationship between oral interview and written narrative when he suggests that the transformation from spoken word into written text is more art than science.[3] In this vein, for clarity's sake and for general coherence, I have at times made minor changes to interviewees' words and phrases, including, but not limited to, in oral historian Alessandro Portelli's cinematic metaphor, cutting, splicing, and shifting.[4] I made every effort to retain the spirit of what was recorded and, as I interpret it, what was intended. I also offered fourteen of the seventeen interviewees an opportunity to review their portions of the narrative during the drafting stages of the writing process.

This is neither a comprehensive nor an impartial history of the Imperial Hotel occupation. Historical work, no matter how good, presents partial and fragmented truths.[5] I have focused on some aspects of the occupation while attending less to others. I have selected particular people to interview while choosing not to interview others. I was specifically charged with writing the history of the Imperial Hotel occupation from the perspective of the Open Door Community and I have shaped the narrative in a way that tells the story of the occupation through their eyes and the eyes of those affiliated with them.

When I began this project, in an effort to push me toward claiming my own voice as a writer and to avoid some of the pitfalls of academic language, Eduard Loring joked that for every footnote I used I would be required to do ten foot-washings at the Open Door. I have relied in large part on primary source material such as oral history interviews and archival records to write this history. Eduard, himself an excellent historian, allowed me access to his highly organized and well-kept records that included documents such as newspaper clippings, meeting minutes, flyers, and photographs. I did not stray too far from Eduard's archival material, but it was at times necessary to seek other sources and to use footnotes, so let the foot washing begin.

INTRODUCTION
PROPHETIC POLITICS IN PHARAOH'S DEN

When reflecting on the role of the 1990 Imperial Hotel occupation in the history of activism in Atlanta, historian Charles Steffen characterized this street action as "redistributive justice," a "crack in the edifice of regime power," a social movement "without precedent," and "one of the most dramatic street actions in Atlanta since the student-led civil rights protests of the 1960s."[6] Steffen is particularly attuned to the leadership role that homeless people played in the occupation:

> The spontaneous mobilization of scores of homeless men, women, and children who found their way to the hotel; the overnight transformation of these homeless people into an organic community engaged in the dual project of physical renovation and political resistance; the rapid consolidation of a leadership team that was authorized to speak for the homeless community as a whole – these made the occupation the single most important example of homeless self-help in Atlanta's history. For sixteen days in the summer of 1990, the most marginalized and dishonored segment of the city's citizenry found its voice, and the most powerful and privileged segment was forced to listen. By any measure, the Imperial Hotel takeover represented the apogee of homeless empowerment.[7]

The Imperial Hotel occupation was never meant to be an occupation; it was intended to be a half-day symbolic protest to bring attention to homelessness and the lack of affordable housing in Atlanta. "The idea was to simply go into the hotel, draw attention, get arrested, and leave," said activist Rev. Houston Wheeler, "but it didn't happen that way."[8]

This book documents, primarily from the perspective of Open Door Community residents and People for Urban Justice activists, the dramatic events that occurred during sixteen remarkable days in June 1990. Founded in 1980, the Open Door Community, a residential Christian community modeled after Catholic Worker houses, performs works of mercy and practices social justice activism.[9] They seek the Beloved Community through loving relationships with neglected outcasts such as homeless people and prisoners. Their works of mercy include providing free meals, showers, haircuts, gently-worn clothes, and a foot clinic. They also publish *Hospitality*, a monthly newspaper, and hold worship services and clarification meetings.[10] Of the "Imperial Eight" – the original eight activists who illegally entered the Imperial Hotel on June 18, 1990 – six were living at the Open Door Community and two were founding members of the community.

In the wake of the Imperial Hotel takeover, affordable housing units *were* developed. Rev. Craig Taylor called it "a lightning strike."[11] Taylor, a long-time advocate for and builder of affordable housing, emphasized that the occupation was the quintessential event in affordable housing development in Atlanta.

When contemplating the role of the Imperial Hotel occupation in the history of street actions in Atlanta, theologian Peter Gathje writes:

> The takeover of the Imperial is perhaps the most dramatic example of the Open Door Community's practice of prophetic politics. This type of politics follows the prophetic tradition in which symbolic acts dramatize realities in conflict with cultural values and thus call people to account. In these symbolic acts the community attempts to point to the societal injustice and suffering that people would prefer to forget or ignore. This political action is grounded in the community's faith.[12]

Theology and justice are interwoven threads that propel and sustain the Open Door's call to action. Under the banner of People for Urban Justice, the 1990 Imperial Hotel occupation illuminates the deep-rooted faith that is manifested daily through acts of hospitality and humility at the Open Door.

People for Urban Justice and the Open Door Community refused to remain idle in the midst of poor people's suffering. They raised their voices and engaged their bodies in "street preaching." According to Theologian Walter Brueggemann, "street preaching, as distinct from conventional church preaching, entails a *willingness to contest and be contested* amidst *bodily reality* . . . Church preaching tends to be safe and consequently innocuous, not because it is in a church building, but because it tends not to be disputatious enough and not be informed by the bodily reality of brokenness so evident on the street."[13] When homeless people and activists from the Open Door and PUJ took to the streets and joined together inside the *bodily reality* of the Imperial Hotel, they intentionally refused to submit to "acceptable" forms of behavior.

The Atlanta Way

In their efforts to promote commerce and to project positive images of race relations, Atlanta's political and business leaders have historically eschewed the kind of violent unrest the world witnessed in Birmingham, Montgomery, and Little Rock. Allowing visible unrest and protest in the streets is not the "Atlanta Way." Atlanta's style is to avoid the *bodily reality* of people striving for justice; instead, civic boosters and the power elite erect façades or apply veneer to image-tarnishing realities. Journalist John Sugg suggests that city and business leaders actively shape particular kinds of narratives about Atlanta: "For many decades [the] clash of narratives has been strangled. It's called the 'Atlanta Way.' Problems are glossed over, people in authority sing 'amen' at the same catechism, and the public is told to wear a happy face. Or else."[14] In the "Atlanta Way" paradigm, the struggles of marginalized people – and the street actions that call attention to them – are hidden from view so that business interests can retain control of the city's image. From a business perspective, what is bad for business is bad for Atlanta.[15]

Another element of the "Atlanta Way" paradigm is that since the late 1940s the traditionally white business elite have absorbed middle-class black leaders into a bi-racial coalition – a powerful and flexible "governing regime" – that harms Atlanta's poor and working-class residents.[16] In *Regime Politics: Governing Atlanta, 1946-1988*, political scientist Clarence Stone argues that the bi-racial governing regime led to regressive public policy in terms of economic development: "It favors the interests of the upper-strata groups and disregards or harms the interests of lower-strata groups."[17] Open Door Community co-founder and self-described street theologian Eduard Loring, who has witnessed the results of Atlanta's public policy more palpably, asserted this more bluntly: Public policy in Atlanta kills poor people. Stone also charged that even though increasing electoral power brought gains to the black middle class, scarce attention was paid to the employment and housing needs of those with limited education and income; as a result, Atlanta was a city of economic extremes.[18]

In *Atlanta: Race, Class, and Urban Expansion*, Larry Keating explains why middle-class blacks collaborated with white business leaders. He also reveals the consequences of this partnership: "Because they gain political and economic benefits from their partnership with the white elite, they have come to share many of the same goals and values. As a consequence, they have paid very little attention to the problems of the city's poor black population." Keating adds: "Even though Atlanta has always had a large population of low-income African Americans, the city's governing coalition did very little to improve their living conditions in the four decades during which the coalition dominated the city's politics. Even after African Americans gained control of city government, black elected officials largely ignored the problems of black poverty."[19] By the late 1980s, when compared to several large U.S. cities, Atlanta was a city of economic extremes and its poverty level was second only to Newark, New Jersey.[20] People of all races experienced this poverty, but Atlanta's African Americans were hit especially hard, as evidenced by creeping economic vulnerability and homelessness.

As they had done before, and as they continue to do today, courageous people affiliated with the Open Door Community exposed the painful and deadly alliances formed and perpetuated through the "Atlanta Way," a governing system that deepened class divisions in a city steeped in racial animosity. The Open Door Community practiced prophetic politics when it raised its voice and engaged in street actions for those who were part of what Houston Wheeler called the "Other" Atlanta:

> Like Jekyll and Hyde, two Atlantas exist as one, but are worlds apart. Looking northward from the Mechanicsville and Summerhill neighborhoods toward the downtown connector, one can gaze at the panorama of modern Atlanta, with its resplendent, gold-domed Capitol, towering new office buildings and hotels,

sleek MARTA rapid transit, gleaming Atlanta-Fulton County Stadium, sober granite government offices and surging urban freeway system. Yet even though Atlanta is a great city of the Southeast, the cost has been that a significant part of Atlanta's population has not prospered. THE OTHER ATLANTA is a city of poor housing, homelessness, under-employment and unemployment."[21]

The Open Door Community continues to seek justice for residents who comprise the "Other" Atlanta – those who are poor, marginalized, and on the receiving end of the "Atlanta Way."

CHAPTER ONE

PREPARING FOR STREET ACTION

People for Urban Justice (PUJ) formed on May 1, 1990. The Imperial Hotel occupation, which began on June 18, was PUJ's first street action. PUJ was a coalition comprised of formerly homeless people, activists affiliated with various social justice groups (including the Open Door Community, Concerned Black Clergy, and Metro Atlanta Task Force for the Homeless), and individuals from the medical, legal, and church advocacy communities of Atlanta.

PUJ's activism began by addressing the abysmal conditions that workers faced at for-profit temporary labor agencies ("labor pools," as they were commonly called). Elizabeth Dede recalled that from the beginning, PUJ was committed to street actions: "We wouldn't just be a group that was having 'butt meetings' (sitting around talking about issues), but instead we would be doing events like guerilla theater."[22] Houston Wheeler indicated, "Our goal was to meet, plan, and organize street actions."

PUJ's actions deliberately took place outside church doors – on the streets, in the neighborhoods, and at city hall and the state capitol. PUJ was certain it would practice *prophetic ministry*, which, according to theologian Walter Brueggemann, aims to "nurture, nourish, and evoke a consciousness and perception alternative to the consciousness and perception of the dominant culture around us."[23]

Drawing inspiration from scripture and from Martin Luther King Jr., PUJ aimed to "contest and be contested amidst [the] bodily reality" of the streets.[24] Murphy Davis explained the beliefs that empowered and emboldened PUJ:

The particular focus of PUJ was around the understanding that to have systemic homelessness is a grave and outrageous sin in the midst of such plenty. We believed that for us not to publicly act out our outrage based on our ministry was sinful. We believed that we had to dramatically call attention to the fact that there was no real reason for homelessness. It was not because Atlanta didn't have enough resources; it was a political decision. It was a mark of the city's political will, and it was wrong. It was dead wrong, and deadly.[25]

Eduard Loring suggested that the spirituality and vision of PUJ came out of the common life and experience of the Open Door Community: "If you read the Open Door's monthly newspaper, *Hospitality*, during the months leading up to the occupation, you find that the theological and practical expressions are exactly the same as those that would be written about and preached about and spoken about under the umbrella of PUJ."[26]

Impetus for Action

The number of homeless people in Atlanta had increased dramatically in the decade leading up to the 1990 Imperial Hotel occupation. In 1984 there were an estimated 3,000 to 5,000 homeless people in Atlanta. That number had risen to an estimated 10,000 to 15,000 by 1989. The Metro Atlanta Task Force for the Homeless estimated that in 1989, 47,000 people spent at least one night in a shelter. During that year there were 80 shelters in metro Atlanta. Forty-three of those shelters were in the city of Atlanta. The total bed capacity metro-wide was 3,200 beds.[27] Clearly, there was an acute deficiency of temporary housing. There was also a severe shortage of affordable long-term housing.

By June of 1990 it was clear that homeless people were facing diminishing odds of finding reasonably priced housing. Activists needed to make their message clear to Atlanta's political leaders, business executives, and residents that this trend was not acceptable. Additionally, their message had to bring attention to the dangerous conditions homeless people encountered on the streets. Merely bringing attention to these problems was not the activists' goal; rather, they sought implementation of policies that would alleviate the housing crisis for Atlanta's poor people.

People for Urban Justice started with labor pool issues, but the closing of the city-run Rising Star Shelter propelled PUJ along a different path. Atlanta's leading political and business figures (including Central Atlanta Progress, a non-profit community development organization headed by business leaders) promoted and partially funded glamorous projects such as sports stadiums for professional teams. One of these projects was Underground Atlanta, a historic five-block area renovated for retail entertainment. By the time Underground Atlanta reopened in 1989, it had cost private and public coffers $142 million.[28] PUJ considered these kinds of developments harmful to Atlanta's people who needed affordable housing. Carol Schlicksup recalled, "Underground Atlanta was a big issue. It was such an expensive, bourgeois place . . . The Imperial Hotel was the opposite of that. Here it was, this hulk of a building standing there empty – not being used by anyone. The city refused to provide housing. We weren't looking for mansions."[29] Growth and development at the cost of disenfranchising Atlanta's poor people frustrated and angered PUJ.

Rising homelessness and the decreasing stock of affordable housing fueled PUJ's activism. Advocates had become involved with the Rising Star Shelter, located where the Georgia Dome (home of the Atlanta Falcons football team) was scheduled to be built. Open Door Community residents and volunteers regularly visited the shelter and delivered bagged lunches. They and others strongly believed that the Georgia Dome construction would devastate African American communities and religious congregations, and would displace poor and homeless people.[30]

Tension in the neighborhood sometimes flared because city police had allowed a large number of homeless folks to have huts nearby. This area, known as "Hutsville," with electricity and a "mayor," was located under the viaduct at the intersection of Martin Luther King Boulevard and Techwood Street. Eduard Loring frequently visited this area and his political consciousness increased, particularly because he and Murphy Davis were members of Concerned Black Clergy, a coalition that had been demonstrating on the streets to protest the Georgia Dome's imminent construction. Murphy said that important coalitions were built during this period among advocates working to improve poor people's lives.

Time and Location

The Imperial Hotel occupation was precipitated by a confluence of various events, including brutal labor pool working conditions, rising numbers of homeless people, a lack of affordable housing, the closing of the Rising Star Shelter, and the first anniversary of the re-opening of Underground Atlanta. Elizabeth Dede said that they were clear they wanted to have an action planned and carried out by the anniversary of the re-opening of Underground. Houston Wheeler recalled:

> The occupation was intentionally designed as a protest to draw attention to the need for affordable housing in view of the city closing the shelter and that monies for affordable housing had been diverted to Underground Atlanta. This was a blatant disregard for the need for affordable housing.
>
> The Open Door had done a lot of protesting with respect to those public monies being diverted toward Underground Atlanta. We wanted to plan an action that would protest the anniversary as well as the closing of the shelter. I think the closing of the shelter was an indication that the city could care less about the homeless. The business community has consistently been about "out of sight, out of mind." They just don't want to see the homeless. Every time you approach them about an issue with respect to the homeless, they don't want to do anything about it. They have other priorities. So that was the context; it was designed as a protest.

Loring's analysis of the occupation suggests that knowing historical context and political milieu is necessary for a better understanding of the urgency in pursuing this particular street action: "I think a point about the intensity of the time and the action around housing was the amount of money that had been spent on Underground Atlanta, and the moral issues of Andy Young and Shirley Franklin and Joe Martin stealing from the poor. And we were quite outraged by that. We still are. Then there was the money for the Georgia Dome, and the Super Bowl was going to be in Atlanta. And so the context had a lot to do with the timing of the action."

Eduard viewed the action from a moral and political perspective when he said, "The moral issue that we have here over and over again is the ludicrous amount of liquid capital, surplus capital, and its misappropriation for entertainment." Throughout Atlanta's recent history, Eduard contends that the entertainment industry, the pursuit of glamorous projects, and the promotion and preservation of national and international image have overshadowed homelessness.

For Sister Jo Ann Geary, a practicing nurse, housing is an essential component of living a healthy life: "Housing is first in everything. If you're going to be healthy you need shelter, and by shelter I mean permanent housing, not shelters as we know them. It's just a basic human right that we provide housing for our people."[31] Like other PUJ members, Jo Ann was critical of the diversion of public monies toward entertainment centers: "People need recreation and entertainment, but there's got to be a balance. If this is how we treat the least of us, that doesn't say very much for us. We have to look at some equality here. Yes, have your entertainment and your pleasures, but let's provide for those less fortunate."

Jo Ann sought to bring attention to the lack of affordable housing to people who were not aware of it, people, for example, in the suburbs who were not exposed to it, or those in the city who did not see it: "We wanted to make a statement with some type of symbolic action to say there's some

The Imperial Hotel in the Atlanta skyline, 1990. Photo courtesy of the Open Door Community

urgency here, there is a big problem and we're not dealing with it." She added, "It's a civil rights issue, it's a justice issue; I think it's just the whole concept of someone is hurting. It is so true: if someone is hurting, we're all hurting, so if there's some way that we can help, alleviate, or lessen that hurt I think that's our responsibility. We're all in this together."

Single-Room-Occupancy Hotels

A significant problem was that single-room-occupancy hotels (SROs) were rapidly dwindling. With rooms letting for roughly seven to ten dollars a night in the 1980s, SROs were a type of no-frills, daily rental hotel room that provided housing for poor people. They helped bridge the gap between the streets and affordable housing; they were converted hotels or new structures built as efficiency apartments with shared kitchens and bathrooms.[32] At SROs, people with a low income, such as those who worked in labor pools or who received disability checks, and often the elderly, could pay daily or weekly. But these affordable places were being, in Murphy's words, "systematically destroyed."

Historian Charles Steffen points out, "It was estimated that twenty-three SRO hotels containing more than 2,000 rooms had been closed or demolished in the downtown area between 1970 and 1986, leaving four run-down establishments clinging to life with a mere 233 rooms among them."[33] Scott Bronstein of the *Atlanta Journal-Constitution* reported that up to 2,000 SRO units had been destroyed through development and that by June 1990 there were less than 1,000 units remaining in the city.[34]

Some of Atlanta's SROs in the 1980s included the Avon Hotel, the Clermont Hotel, the Falcon, the Mitchell Street, the Ponce de Leon, the Scoville, the Shady Rest, and the St. Francis. The Imperial Hotel was at one time an SRO. "So it was very specific," Murphy reported. "When we said 'House the Homeless Here!' it wasn't like a new idea; it was the kind of place where people who were homeless had lived, and they lived there because they could afford to. You could work out of a labor pool and afford a place like the Imperial."

Stanley Gibson, a homeless person who participated in the Imperial Hotel occupation, remembered that SROs were an important housing option for low-wage workers: "It wasn't very much to rent a room for the night. I can't remember the cost exactly, but it was affordable, and that was the main thing."[35]

Stanley also believed that a room at an SRO helped get people off the streets: "It was like a stepping stone. It was a place to start. It was a base of operations. You could get yourself focused, get your money going, have a place inside with running water, a place to sleep that was safe, and then go ahead and move to the next phase."

Stanley Gibson at the Open Door Community, 2005. Photo by author.

Robert Dobbins at the Open Door Community, 2005. Photo by author.

"By the time the Imperial Hotel occupation was going on," explained Robert Dobbins, a labor pool worker and homeless person who also participated in the occupation, "the most boomin' jobs was the labor pools."[36] The men and women who used labor pools sold their labor for a pittance while the agencies profited from the workers' long hours and low pay. While Atlanta boomed, low-wage workers suffered. With only fifteen to twenty-five dollars in their hands for a long day's work, labor pool workers could not afford housing with a long-term rental agreement and security deposit, but they could afford ten bucks for a room in an SRO.

Class Matters: SROs in Neighborhoods

Classism prevented SRO development in some neighborhoods. A July 7, 1990, editorial in the *Atlanta Journal-Constitution* discussed the political geography of affordable housing: "The neighborhoods – and their City Council members – must be made to accept SROs in their back yards. Too often, housing for the poor follows the path of least resistance and ends up squashed together in the middle of nowhere." The writer opined: "A new social compact is needed, where all city neighborhoods agree to shoulder their fair share." Some of this development had already started: in the Summerhill neighborhood, a 60-room SRO at Bethlehem Baptist Church (the Bethlehem Inn) was being prepared for non-profit redevelopment, with rooms expected to rent at $50 a week. The writer pushed Mayor Jackson to commit time and personnel, and spirited words concluded the letter: "It's time to get cracking."[37]

Historically, single-room-occupancy hotels provided economical lodging for traveling salespersons. More recently, they served as temporary affordable housing for labor pool workers and itinerant workers. By the early 1990s, SROs were enjoying a renaissance across the country, but not in Atlanta. Destruction of more than two thousand SRO units was implemented in the decades leading up to the Imperial Hotel occupation. Less than a thousand remained in Atlanta. There was no shortage of SRO proposals from private and non-profit groups, but financing, site selection, and community acceptance were the biggest hurdles.[38] Community approval was a significant problem, because by the early 1990s in Atlanta and across the United States, attitudes about homelessness had generally shifted from compassion to impatience.[39]

Compassion was certainly absent in Atlanta when Lake Claire residents successfully opposed a planned SRO hotel in their neighborhood in 1990. Lake Claire resident Jane Wright was considered a "champion of many worthy causes." She felt powerfully about literacy, education, and safety in neighborhoods, but when a developer tried to build an SRO in her neighborhood, she helped lead the battle that defeated the proposal. "I have yet to see an SRO that hasn't created problems for the neighborhoods that surround them," she said.[40]

"Every project is going to be an uphill battle," said Richard Bradfield, the architect who designed the Lake Claire building. He added, "People are still prejudiced, not just racially, but economically. We can try to educate people, but we're never going to overcome fear of the unknown."[41] Bruce Gunter, a developer of affordable housing, suggested that critics of SROs "use code words because they don't want to be called racist or classist, but . . . that's what it comes down to."[42]

A common perception was that SROs were flophouses with unemployed men hanging around.[43] Of the fewer than 1,000 SRO units that remained in Atlanta, most were in shabby, aging hotels that reinforced negative stereotypes. But newer SROs were different: some boasted on-site security and management, neatly landscaped yards, cleaning services and furnished, carpeted rooms. The Stratford Inn, opened in 1990 on North Avenue near downtown, was a Mediterranean-style building with a two-story atrium in the lobby.[44] Woody Bartlett, program director for Atlanta's Corporation for Supportive Housing, pointed out that despite apprehension from surrounding neighbors who believed having formerly homeless neighbors nearby escalated crime and reduced property values, the refurbished and freshly landscaped properties often raised surrounding real estate values, especially when tenants were carefully screened to ensure their success.[45]

Legislation had been discussed to restrict SROs to commercial areas, but advocates and some city officials believed SROs should be located throughout Atlanta. Bill Holland, statewide coordinator for the Task Force for the Homeless, said that it would require political toughness, but "once the decision is made to go in, it's amazing how the passions die down," referring to opposition that flared and then fizzled over the development of the Stratford Inn.[46] City Councilwoman Barbara Asher indicated that acceptance of SROs required community education: "What you try and do is sit down with people in the neighborhood and people managing the facility and try to get good-neighbor commitments on both parts."[47] Stratford Inn architect Richard Bradfield remained upbeat when he exclaimed, "I think when we get two or three facilities up and operating, we're going to find people who say this isn't so bad."[48]

Land was cheaper on Atlanta's south side but it was not fair for those residents to bear the burden for the entire city. Southwest Atlanta residents voiced their concerns because they believed that developers would prey upon their neighborhoods. "SROs could be nice or they could become flophouses. And we know who's going to get them – neighborhoods south of the city's north-south line," said an opponent. A developer responded: "I'm trying to foster and promote the type of housing we need in our city . . . SROs are a very important type of housing. But they need to be available all over the city."[49]

Prejudice was apparent in the development of the Walton House, a former hotel in the Fairlie-Poplar district of downtown Atlanta. In 1988, the hotel housed dignitaries attending the Democratic National Convention in Atlanta. It had fallen into serious financial trouble, and in 1991 Progressive Redevelopment, Inc. (PRI) bought the building for $1 million. In an effort to gain some political muscle to shore up funding for renovation, PRI partnered with Antioch Baptist Church North, a congregation that held influence in the city's administration. They put together a package of funding to convert the building into an SRO for working homeless people and people who were recovering from serious illnesses, including HIV and TB. Downtown business leaders resisted the idea. They believed an SRO of this kind would not be good for the mixed-use commercial and residential zone they were striving for in the Fairlie-Poplar District. They actively recruited middle-class adults and Georgia State University students to the neighborhood.[50]

Downtown business leaders objected to the idea of having people with HIV live in the area. "That just really made everybody bananas," Joe Beasley recalled.[51] He was human resources director at Antioch. He witnessed people's outrage when they realized that not only would poor people live at the proposed site, but some of those poor people would be ill. From their point of view the neighborhood would become "polluted." A city leader stated, "Putting that facility in Fairlie-Poplar would be tantamount to putting a toxic waste dump in your front yard."[52] Central Atlanta Progress (CAP) president Lewis Holland remarked, "It would become a hospice. I don't think that is the location for a hospice."[53] Beasley responded by saying that the downtown business community was "out of touch with human reality."[54] Bruce Gunter of Progressive Redevelopment exclaimed, "Their vision of Fairlie-Poplar is sidewalk cafes with Cinzano umbrellas, but we are trying to respond to a problem that no one else is responding to. I think the two could co-exist."[55]

CAP convinced Mayor Jackson that Fairlie-Poplar was not a good location for the Walton House SRO, so he withdrew his support. The lender, BankSouth, had a last-minute change of heart about financing renovation of the building. A bank representative said that the decision was based on potential repayment of the loan, and was therefore a business decision and not a political one. In what appeared to be an effort at image control, CAP said they would be interested in purchasing the Walton building if another location was found for an SRO.[56]

An editorial printed in the *Atlanta Journal* revealed the context in which discussions about the Walton building occurred. The writer's liberal, status-quo point of view reminds us why revitalization often displaces poor people:

> The apparent breakdown in financing for a single-room-occupancy hotel in Atlanta's Fairlie-Poplar district ought to be reason for its sponsors, the city and the business community to take deep breaths, ratchet down the gears and rest for a minute. Enough objections have been raised – about purchase and start-up funds, about operating costs and about just what the Walton House will become – to warrant more careful consideration. Mayor Maynard Jackson rushed to announce the project only

to see one source of financing withdrawn. Officials of Antioch Baptist Church North claim to see the invisible hand of the business community behind the opposition to the project and they question the motivation. In fact, speaking for downtown businesses, Central Atlanta Progress has proposed a task force to find alternative sites for the facility for the working poor and those who exist through downtown day-labor centers. CAP chief Lewis Holland isn't opposed to an SRO for the working poor, but worries that Walton House might also open its doors to drug-abusers and others. CAP has promised to help raise funds should an alternative site be identified.

Neither side is wrong in this effort. Housing for the working poor is needed badly. The Walton site might be the best. But an overriding interest for all Atlantans is the strength of downtown. For years, Fairlie-Poplar has been the focus of intense revitalization efforts. Those efforts should not be written off, for as Five Points wavers, Fairlie-Poplar becomes all the more important. It should be remembered that an exodus is underway. Wachovia Bank is moving north on Peachtree, to be followed by NationsBank. A slew of large law firms preceded them. The Walton House project arises just as sensitive negotiations with Georgia State University are bearing fruit. If the university can be persuaded, the edge of Five Points could become the center for the school's performing and visual arts facilities. Hotels now used in part as halfway houses for former convicts could become student housing. Who eventually lives in Walton House at the other end of Fairlie-Poplar is important. The principals in the discussion would do well to discuss and encourage alternative sites as well as exactly who might live in Walton House if it gets a green light. The issue isn't one of rich and poor or black and white. It is the economic health of the city's core.[57]

For this writer, the "economic health" of the city was more important than providing housing for Atlanta's poor and vulnerable residents. It is reasonable to desire thriving businesses in a downtown business district, but to attempt to retain business at any cost is a slippery slope toward a cruel society. As is often the case, revitalization produces "winners" and "losers." Poor people, of course, are nearly always on the losing end of these deals. Down but not out, Beasley declared:

> They thought they had us dead because of Central Atlanta Progress and the Chamber of Commerce and all of these dynamics that had been playing for a number of months when they knew we had control of the building. Central Atlanta Progress said if we were going to get control of that building then it would completely kill Fairlie-Poplar. "People are not going to live around poor people," they said. They even made the statement that having an SRO in Fairlie-Poplar is like having a garbage dump in a community. But it energized us more. We had moral authority.

Beasley contended that even though Mayor Jackson initially supported the Walton House conversion to an SRO, business interests swayed him to change his mind. Bitterly, Joe said, "He had pledged to build 3,500 units and this would be part of his commitment. But he didn't want it because the business community determined 'this is just not going to fit; it's not going to work.'"

Eventually, Mayor Jackson went against CAP's wishes: he convened a 10:00 p.m. press conference (in time for the 11:00 p.m. news) on the front steps of the Walton to announce his support for the deal, and the city money that went with it. Earlier, PRI board member Rev. Timothy McDonald led a protest against BankSouth by passing out $1 checks for people to present to the bank tellers at their branch on Peachtree Street. BankSouth reneged on the deal with PRI and Antioch, but the next bank did not: First Union agreed to sponsor the loan request to the Federal Home Loan Bank, and considerable money was raised for the renovation.[58]

Despite the initial resistance to an SRO in the Fairlie-Poplar district, persistence, propelled by PRI's technical know-how and Antioch's political muscle, paid dividends. The Walton House, previously an 88-room hotel, opened as a 128-unit SRO in 1993. Additionally, Craig Taylor and PRI responded to CAP's concerns about people living with HIV in the area by successfully negotiating for a donated building that housed people living with HIV in a different neighborhood. Through a non-profit that Taylor named the Cooperative Resource Center, the donated building was renovated and eventually opened with 46 SRO units.[59] After the storm of controversy subsided about the potential residents of Walton House, Atlanta Chamber of Commerce president Gerald Bartels acknowledged that the business community had overreacted in their opposition to it.[60]

The Imperial Hotel

Built in 1910 and opened in 1911 at the corner of Peachtree Street and Ralph McGill Boulevard, at the north edge of Atlanta's central business district, the eight-story Imperial Hotel began its life as a traditional hotel that catered to businessmen, conventioneers, and tourists.[61] The Imperial was not fancy, but it was considered respectably middle class.[62] In the 1950s and 1960s, famous jazz and blues artists played in the hotel's club, the Domino Lounge. In the 1970s the Imperial's stature dropped significantly: the hotel eventually became a flophouse, and the club featured adult entertainment and exotic dancers. Neglect and disrepair characterized the Imperial's downhill trajectory in the late 1970s.[63] Reflecting on a visit Murphy and Eduard made to some friends staying at the Imperial in the 1970s, Murphy said, "It was a dump. It was a dive. All kinds of stuff went on there. But it was a roof, for heaven's sake. It was not elegant housing, but it was warm and dry, and people had shelter there."

Karen D., a Detroit native who moved to Atlanta as a teenager in 1972, frequented the Imperial Hotel in the mid-1970s. She was part of a drug culture that formed at the Domino Lounge. Karen, currently a college professor, drew from Greek mythology to clarify her reflections about her

The Imperial Hotel, ca. 1920. Photo courtesy of the Kenan Research Center at the Atlanta History Center.

time at the Imperial: "I would describe it like Virgil's epic Latin poem, *The Aeneid,* when Aeneis is going into the underworld and he sees all of the woes and evil of humankind at the entrance of the underworld – that was what the Imperial represented; it was the worst side of the drugs, sex, and rock-n-roll culture."[64] She recalled that at that time, seven to ten dollars a night for a room was a sizeable amount of money because minimum wage was about $1.75 an hour. She believes that labor pool workers certainly could have been using the hotel as a place to sleep or, as Stanley Gibson suggests, a "stepping stone to something else." "It certainly wasn't the bottom," Karen explained.

Karen remembered the burlesque shows in the Domino Lounge and drew a striking analogy between human activities inside the hotel and its physical condition: "What I remember is seeing women that worked in the lounge who were burlesque performers, but with that came the prostitution upstairs. And I also remember some aging women, and I don't really know their story, but I remember the corridor smelled like old booze and cheap perfume, and you could tell that at one time it had been plush and regal and that it had just slid into disrepair." Karen described the general atmosphere of the hotel as a place where sadness permeated everything, adding, "I'm sure in its heyday it was a very nice place. You could see that at one time people were happy there, and the place where it is situated in Atlanta is so central to everything, but it was forgotten."

The Imperial Hotel closed its doors for business in 1980. Atlanta architect and developer John Portman purchased it in 1986. As older buildings receded in the shadows of Atlanta's growing skyline of modern buildings, Portman probably intended to raze the Imperial Hotel. Charles Steffen wrote:

> The eighty-year-old structure was among the SROs that had fallen victim to commercial real estate development. It stood forlornly at the gateway of architect-developer John Portman's Peachtree Center, a modernist complex of hotels, office towers, and shopping malls, connected by pedestrian skyways that floated above the disorder of the streets. In Portman's mind, the Imperial Hotel symbolized an outmoded past, Peachtree Center an irresistible future. When he bought the Imperial in 1986, he

bolted the doors and let time take its toll, waiting for the right moment to clear the site for redevelopment.[65]

Preparing for Action

The goal to break into the Imperial was a lofty one because it gave PUJ only six weeks to prepare. Elizabeth Dede explained: "I would say that part of the spirituality of the Open Door Community was a very clear calling to action. And not just to prayer and faith. We believed our actions had to have feet." Carol Schlicksup welcomed the opportunity to engage in street actions. The Open Door, she said, *is* action. But, according to Carol, "This was a new piece . . . To take this step was a much more active involvement in the battle, and I welcomed that." Even though PUJ members had been involved in street actions and even slept on the street at various times during the year, this was another step; this was a direct violation – it was trespassing.

Sister Jo Ann Geary knew it would be breaking the law, but she did not hesitate. She had been arrested before, and this was just one more act of civil disobedience. She believed there was a risk of arrest, but it was worth it because housing issues needed to be addressed, and this was one way to do it. As a form of street preaching, she felt that this was an important action, especially because the reality of the streets was not addressed in churches. For Jo Ann, churches had become too institutionalized and too concerned with the law rather than the spirit. However, she was concerned about John Flournoy, C.M. Sherman, and Larry Travick, the formerly homeless participants comprising the "Imperial Eight"; she wondered if it might be more difficult for them to deal with such serious legal charges, especially if they already had a criminal record.

According to Elizabeth, the process from thinking about the action to doing the action was quite short – probably only two weeks. She said: "I think Eduard came up with the idea. We had been planning for several weeks to go back to Underground Atlanta to do something there on the one-year anniversary. And then Eduard came up with the idea of the takeover of the Imperial Hotel, and we all believed that this would be a much more dramatic action."

Dick Rustay, Murphy and Eduard's friend since 1980, had been living with his wife, Gladys, at the Open Door for just over eight months prior to the June occupation. Dick recalled that PUJ did a lot of preliminary work to prepare for their entry into the hotel.[66] Members scouted the hotel to see what would be necessary to enter the building, and after learning that there was a chain on the front door, they acquired a large cutter to break it. They decided when people would enter the building, and they made the three-by-twenty-foot banner that they planned to place near the roof which said "House the Homeless Here!" And they notified news agencies.

The year before, for the action at Underground Atlanta, they had consulted with an attorney to better understand the consequences of getting arrested during a protest, so they understood that element, and they were prepared for that.

In some ways, Carol reasoned, it was very simple: PUJ and the Open Door shared the same goals, and PUJ was taking one more step with this action on the street, one that was more dangerous and uncertain than previous actions. As she rode in the van with the group to the Imperial just before four o'clock in the morning, she was contemplating the impending danger. She recalled getting the sense that others in the van were also thinking about the potential danger: "I know I did. I thought this could be a little dangerous, a little scary, but then there was a certain excitement about taking a step – a certain release to doing that, like finally, one more step out into the reality of Atlanta's mistreatment of and injustice toward the poor."

Carol had known about liberation theology prior to the occupation, and Eduard had brought the idea of liberation theology to PUJ discussions. As she rode in the van to the hotel, and PUJ prepared to break the chains on the hotel door, Carol was living liberation theology. The British Broadcasting Corporation defines the movement, which was opposed by Pope John Paul II, in this way:

> Liberation theology was a radical movement that grew up in South America as a response to the poverty and the ill-treatment of ordinary people. The movement was caricatured in the phrase *If Jesus Christ were on Earth today, he would be a Marxist revolutionary*, but it's more accurately encapsulated in this paragraph from Leonardo and Clodovis Boff:
>
> Q: How are we to be Christians in a world of destitution and injustice?

A: There can be only one answer: we can be followers of Jesus and true Christians only by making common cause with the poor and working out the gospel of liberation.

Liberation theology said the church should derive its legitimacy and theology by growing out of the poor. The Bible should be read and experienced from the perspective of the poor.[67]

CHAPTER TWO
BREAKING THE CHAIN

The Imperial Hotel takeover was not originally designed as an occupation. The event was planned as a half-day street action. The activists were certain they would be arrested and taken to jail, and then it would be over. They expected to be back at the Open Door Community in the early afternoon. The primary goal was to hang the banner on the hotel with the aim of getting media and news agencies engaged. The geographical location for the action was important: the Imperial was in a highly traversed route on Peachtree Street in the corridor between downtown and midtown. If everything went as planned, the action would bring urgent attention to homelessness in Atlanta.

Prior to breaking in, PUJ had assigned roles to each of the members. Houston Wheeler explained, "We didn't all go into the hotel initially, but we agreed to meet there at a certain time after breaking in." When asked why all PUJ members did not enter the building initially, Houston recalled, "Everybody had a particular role. I think the concern was that we didn't want to have a lot of people arrested. Different actions call for different goals and I think that the main goal was for those six or seven people to get arrested and draw attention to the need for affordable housing and to protest the city's priorities."

The activists determined that they did not want a throng of people at the door of the Imperial when they were breaking the chains, fearing that this would bring unwanted attention. They suspected that John Portman's security staff would be nearby, because his company had a large project underway in the immediate area.

They did a rehearsal early Sunday morning, June 17. Around three o'clock, the activists drove a van to the hotel to determine if police were in the area. They decided to use Elizabeth Dede and Don Beisswenger as decoys to draw attention away from the hotel if police officers or security guards arrived. The plan, Elizabeth explained, was that she and Don would stay in the van parked across the street from the Imperial, and if the police came, they would start shouting at each other so the police would come over to find out what the shouting was about and she and Don would tell them they were a married couple having a fight. Looking back at the event, Elizabeth chuckled and said, "I was just about young enough to be Don's granddaughter."

As some of the activists waited and watched from across the street while the chain was being broken, Carol Schlicksup realized that they were under the street lights much longer than expected. They were certain that Portman's security staff saw people milling about the hotel when they patrolled the area. Oddly enough, the security staff did not do anything about it.

With the others on lookout, C.M. Sherman cut the chain and removed it. He threw the chain and lock into a trash can. They had brought their own chain and lock which they put on the door. Once it was done, they got back into the van and went to Dunk-N-Dine for breakfast.

Roughly twenty-four hours later, the activists did a second and final run to the hotel. Between 3:00 and 4:00 a.m., Don drove the van that shuttled the activists to a location near the Imperial. They circled up and prayed before they opened the lock, removed the chain, and went in. They were surprised at how easy it had been to break into the abandoned hotel.

First Few Hours

Getting inside the hotel was risky, and the activists knew they were breaking the law. Murphy Davis said, "It was really upping the ante. We had never done anything like cutting a chain to enter." The activists had committed a crime – trespassing – and they knew they would suffer harsh consequences upon their arrest.

After they entered the hotel, Carol remembers that it was dark, with a labyrinth of steps and hallways. They did not know if there was anybody else

Left: Supporters of the Imperial Hotel action march on the streets near the hotel on the first day of the action. Photo courtesy of the Open Door Community.

Above: Supporters of People for Urban Justice hold a banner emphasizing their concerns, from left, Rev. Nibs Stroupe, Phillip Williams, unknown, Dick Rustay, and Ed Potts. Photo courtesy of the Open Door Community.

in the hotel, which was a frightening idea. At first everyone stayed together, and then gradually some people scouted ahead. The building was dilapidated and Eduard recalled that it was especially scary to go up the stairs in the dark. Murphy added, "It was creepy. We had no flashlights. We didn't want to risk any light shining through a window."

They did not want to be discovered and arrested before the public action. "We were so scared of the police," Eduard recalled. Murphy said that he was a "basket case of anxiety." Eduard admitted that he was tense: "Well, I was. We thought that this was really going to be an important action."

The protesters knew that the hotel would be filthy inside. Murphy and Eduard recalled being in the hotel in the early to mid-1980s when it was officially unoccupied. During that time people could enter through a fire escape, and people were routinely doing that and "catting" everywhere (creating temporary resting spots wherever they could find them – in abandoned buildings, under bridges, etc.). The fire escape was eventually removed so that people could not enter, but because of the earlier occupants, the place was a mess. Murphy pointed out, "We knew that it was going to be really filthy, with a lingering presence of people who'd lived there and had food there and used it as a bathroom and all of those kinds of things." She described the scene inside when they arrived for the action: "We knew that we were not going into a pretty sight. In fact it was trashed. The whole thing was trashed. Windows were broken. It had been sitting idle for a number of years by that time. I don't think we had any real surprises about that. We knew there would be rats and there were. We knew there would be broken glass and there was. We knew there would be a lot of leftover human waste and there was."

Elizabeth recalled that they all wore big boots to guard against broken glass inside, and she remembered hearing rats scurrying across the floors. Jo Ann Geary confirmed that they had to be careful because it was in total disarray, with debris all over the floors and toilets turned over on their side.

Not long after they entered the hotel, the activists went up to the roof of the building, but they did not stay long. Under Eduard's urging, they quickly stepped down from the roof because he realized that crane operators would begin working soon, and he believed they were hired by security companies to keep watch over the area. The activists figured that if the crane operators saw them on the roof, they would likely report them to Portman's security guards and to the Atlanta city police, and they did not want to get arrested before they had a chance to hang the banner.

Elizabeth remembered that they went to a lower floor where they got into inner hallways so they could not be seen from the outside. They intended to be discovered by the police, but not yet. Eduard was more cautious and concerned than everyone else. At Sacred Heart Catholic Church next door, roofers began work around 6:00 a.m. Elizabeth recalled that Eduard was certain they could see the protesters. "It was absurd," Murphy exclaimed.

Murphy Davis and Eduard Loring at the Imperial Hotel on the first day of the action. Photo courtesy of the Open Door Community.

Sister Jo Ann Geary, left, and Sister Carol Schlicksup in the Imperial Hotel on the first day of the action. Photo courtesy of the Open Door Community.

Eduard admitted that he was paranoid about getting caught and that he might have overreacted in those early morning hours. But, more important, he learned a lot about social class during the first few hours of the action: "We got in touch with something we've experienced at the Open Door over the years in terms of the difference of class: when those of us who are educated and middle class land in jail we sit around and worry, but people from the streets go to sleep." Murphy agreed: "None of the white folks slept a wink that morning." The PUJ activists who had previously been homeless – C.M. Sherman, Larry Travick, and John Flournoy – slept soundly after they entered the hotel. So deeply, in fact, they snored. Eduard feared that the noise would draw attention to the building, and he fretted about changes at the parking lot near the building: "We were aware when the business of the day would begin and we knew people would start driving by. We wondered if they would know the chains were different and that we were inside."

The group was surprised by how the day was unfolding. Houston Wheeler remembered those early morning hours: "What they would do is have guards come by periodically, a security company or something like that. I think by five o'clock in the morning or so they had a security guard that ignored us. He didn't call the police or do anything to have anybody arrested."

Hanging the Banner

The protesters were planning to hang the banner at 11:00 a.m. so they could get media attention for the noon television news broadcast. It was a long wait after having entered the hotel at four. Murphy remembered that it seemed like an endless number of hours. Eduard read the Bible. Some people ate snacks.

While it was still dark, Elizabeth and others explored the hotel to see which floors and windows would provide the best views for the impending action. They had already decided they would hang the banner on the top floor, just under the Imperial sign.

PUJ activists and Open Door residents were asked to arrive at the hotel around nine o'clock. Because they planned to march in front of the hotel, they brought protest signs. They entered the building and joined the eight other activists. They waited together for eleven o'clock, when the banner was to be displayed.

Murphy explained how they hung the banner: "Some of us went into one bay window and some of us into the other. We had sticks that we reached across and we had rope." The banner was unfurled and, down below at street level, activists marched as the banner greeted Atlanta's skyline: "House the Homeless Here!"

The activists hoped the sign would alert Atlanta's middle-class people to the struggles of Atlanta's poor and homeless people. To their dismay, after hanging the banner, they realized it was not nearly large enough. Murphy recalled, "It looked like a little Band-Aid way up there. It was just pitiful."

The banner had been professionally made, and Elizabeth had asked the printers to create the largest size possible. Dick Rustay chuckled as he recalled how diminutive the sign looked: "We thought it was huge, but it looked really small up there."

Carol believed the banner was an integral part of the occupation, despite its small size: "That was so important, because otherwise people would drive by and wouldn't notice what was going on. The message made it obvious that there was some kind of an occupation happening."

After they hung the banner, Eduard shouted through a megaphone to the crowd below: "We ask right now for Maynard Jackson to come up here with us. Last year we built Underground Atlanta; this year let's build housing above ground for human beings."

The Imperial Hotel on the first day of the action after the "House the Homeless Here" banner was unfurled. Photo courtesy of the Open Door Community.

In an effort to get more people involved in the street action, Gladys Rustay and others from the Open Door went to the nearby Episcopal Church, where they knew a meal was being served to several hundred homeless people.[68] Gladys recalled that it was more difficult than expected to get people to join them in the march from the church to the hotel. She was shocked because, as she viewed it, the march was for them; however, she later realized that not only were some of the homeless people concerned about getting arrested, but also, since the Open Door Community had been open for only ten years at that time, there was not as great a sense of trust among the homeless community for the Open Door and its actions as there was in later years. Despite the low turnout from the church, roughly 35 Open Door residents and volunteers (Gladys's son among them) marched on the street in front of the hotel. The marchers spaced themselves out so that it might look as if there were more people involved in the protest.

PUJ had notified newspapers and television stations about the event, but they waited in vain for the press to arrive. The plan was for the action to garner some media attention, the

The "Imperial Eight" of People for Urban Justice hanging the "House the Homeless Here" banner on the Imperial Hotel. Photo courtesy of the Open Door Community.

PUJ folk to get arrested, and everyone to be out of the building by early afternoon. "What we had planned just didn't happen. The press didn't accumulate. The police didn't come," Murphy commented. "It was, 'What do we do now?' And we really didn't know what we were going to do. We didn't have a plan B."

Dick Rustay was surprised, even a bit unnerved, about how the day was unfolding. He believed that the hotel guard saw the banner on the side of the building and the protesters marching in front of the hotel. But for some reason the guard decided not to disrupt the action: "We were marching and people looked at us as if we were crazy, with our signs about housing the homeless and the cost of Underground Atlanta. We thought that the folks inside would be arrested, and then we'd finish and go back to the Open Door."

Gladys Rustay was alarmed when she saw that people were not paying attention. "What are those fools doing?" she imagined people were thinking. The participants were disappointed, especially because they had gotten so energized for the action. Jo Ann Geary thought, "What's going on? What does this mean? Do they think we're just going to go away if they ignore us?" She wanted people to pay attention; she wanted the action to have meaning.

Around noon it was clear that their protest was not going to happen as they had planned. Inattention to protests and protesters is a theme that has dogged Open Door activism over the years, Eduard revealed. Failure to respond, he added, is "typical of mainline, status quo Christians who do not have the courage to put their bodies on the line for justice."

"There is an arc in the universe and it bends toward justice," Martin Luther King Jr. and others have charged. Events were not turning out as PUJ had planned, but maybe there was a larger, more powerful force at play.

"House the Homeless Here" banner on the Imperial Hotel. Photo courtesy of the Open Door Community.

After PUJ entered the hotel and raised the banner, homeless people did eventually begin congregating outside the hotel. The Imperial was near a bridge that crossed Interstate 75/85, a well-traveled path for homeless folks who were going to St. Luke's soup kitchen.

The homeless people joined others on the street carrying signs and banners that brought attention to the economic injustice they perceived in Atlanta's affordable housing shortage. Eduard called these others the "radical remnant": the moral and ethical supporters of PUJ and the Open Door Community who did not live at the Open Door but joined them in street actions. According to social critic Michael Eric Dyson, the radical remnant – originating in the black church and informing Martin Luther King Jr. – drew upon a theology of justice and liberation. Dyson writes:

> King was profoundly influenced by the militant minority of the black Baptist church. He readily took to its theology of love – not the sappy, sentimental emotion but the demanding, disciplined practice of social charity – and to its theology of racial justice and social liberation. Since the church was at the heart of the black community's resistance to racism, King's efforts to transform American society were founded on his prophetic faith. The radical remnant – or, as I use them here interchangeably, the prophetic brigade or militant minority – of the black church taught King how to translate his faith into the language of social justice and civic virtue.[69]

The people marching in solidarity in front of the hotel – this militant minority resisting the status quo, this prophetic brigade embodying activist Christian theology – formed a radical remnant by raising their voices and putting their bodies on the line for social justice and civic virtue.

CHAPTER THREE
OPENING THE DOOR

In the early afternoon of Monday, June 18, Eduard went to the street, where now many homeless people were gathered. Sheri Finch, a photographer for the *Gwinnett Daily News*, stood with Houston Wheeler, PUJ's designated media contact. Houston introduced Eduard to Sheri. She wanted to go inside the hotel, but Eduard would not allow her to enter, since the activists inside had agreed that they were not going to open the door to anyone. Finch persisted and, after talking with Houston, Eduard acquiesced.

Eduard explained, "Well, our action had failed, and she wanted to come in. She wanted to make a story about this place. So I opened the door and let her in. And then I took her upstairs and ran into Murphy. And I got one of my calls to accountability, which was right. I had made a decision that was not processed through the group. I had acted as an individualist; I was the male in control. And Murphy was pretty pissed."

Elizabeth Dede was also at the front door with Finch and Eduard, but she remembered this incident differently and said that she and Eduard *both* made the decision to let Finch inside the hotel. This decision – to allow the journalist into the hotel – signaled one of the complications associated with activism. Eduard illustrated:

> It's one of the real problems of front-line leadership. We were in this hotel and nothing that we had planned, worked. There was no response, and here was a press person really wanting to get in and saying that she would take some pictures and write some stories. At that point it is always a problem, and it is an important

problem, and one that cannot be easily dismissed. But the tension is, do you go through a process that takes time and may make this person lose interest? You balance those competing interests. And I really am quite pleased to hear that Elizabeth was there because my impression was I made that decision all alone.

Eduard's decision to let someone into the hotel without group approval stirred him to comment on another Open Door principle:

One principle that we try to live by at the Open Door is that we don't offer for one what we don't offer for all. We opened the door to Sheri Finch, but perhaps if there were more press asking to get in then maybe we would have opened the door for all of them. At that time we weren't going to let in friends from Butler Street Breakfast or somebody that came to 910 or lived in our yard. The answer was No to them. So at the point that we first opened the door and let one press person in, that was not only a violation of a process of sharing authority and decision-making, it was also breaking a principle that we try to live by.

Murphy and Eduard disagreed over how to proceed once the hotel had been breached. Eduard wanted to open the door to homeless people, but Murphy wanted to wait longer and think it through more thoroughly. She recalled her thoughts at the time: "We all needed to be together on what we were doing because this was going to be a big change. So we got together and made the joint decision to open the front door, and folks started milling around and coming in."

Once they decided to let the homeless folks in, it was clear that they were taking on something very big. And even though the decision to let the journalist in caused a rift among the activists, Murphy did not give up on the idea of making collaborative decisions: "It's an important thing to talk about from the get-go because in a situation like that you are inventing it every second. It's an unrelentingly creative act in a political action like ours."

Some residents of the Open Door and some people who were part of the radical remnant also entered the hotel when the homeless folks began arriving. Murphy described the scene: "It was the Open Door residential community and whoever else came along, and Houston, our designated press person.

Frances Pauley was there, and Lewis Sinclair. Frances held a sign that said 'Where Will You Sleep Tonight?'"

Eduard considered the moment *kairos* when they opened the hotel door and welcomed others to enter. In Greek mythology, Kairos, Zeus's youngest child, was the God of opportunity. In classical rhetoric, kairos suggests the seizing of an opportune time or place, "a passing instant when an opening appears which must be driven through with force if success is to be achieved."[70] In Christianity, Christ is said to have come *en kairo*, sometimes translated as "'the fullness of time' – implying a culmination in a temporal development marked by the manifestation of God in an actual historical order."[71]

Eduard realized that this moment was kairos: an opening had appeared and the moment needed to be seized – time and destiny had collided, and it was a situation rich with possibility. The day's events were a symbolic action and the activists realized that the time had come to maximize the opportunity that it opened for them. Reflecting on the decision to let people in, Eduard said, "It could have been disastrous, but it wasn't. It's a risk, but it's a risk that you take in all that you do." Opening the door to others was a transition point, and nobody knew what would happen next.

It was clear that opening the door to homeless people would significantly alter the dynamics and nature of the occupation. Murphy believed that it would be a loss of control:

> To open the door was to say, "We don't know who will come in, we don't know how many people will come in, and we don't know what kind of issues and agenda people will bring with them." When you're talking about opening a door and just letting things flow you are talking about a lot of different kinds of issues. Some folks have really got their heads on straight. Some folks are really together and are going to cooperate and be supportive. And then among the homeless you always have people who have serious chemical addictions and varying levels of mental illness. So you just don't know what's going to be the strongest dynamic in that.

In addition to the potential change in individual and group dynamics, Elizabeth began to consider the physical and material needs that would be required if they opened the door to homeless folks and if anybody was to stay much longer: bathrooms, water, light, and food. Murphy, too, recalled that the bathroom situation was one of the first issues they had to deal with, especially because so many people entered the hotel: "We couldn't all just go down the hall into an empty room and do whatever we wanted – it became a matter of a lot of people very quickly."

For Eduard, the decision to open the door to homeless folks reflected the history of the Open Door's faithfulness to hospitality among Atlanta's poor, homeless, and African American populations:

> One of the things that happened over our years since the Open Door started has been, slowly, the development of trust and moral authority between the Open Door and many homeless people, predominately male and predominately black. And there are several reasons for that. One of them is that we live at 910, and we do not live luxuriously. Anybody who knows us and has been in the house knows that we don't make money off the homeless. Another reason has been the Butler Street Breakfast, and the breakfast here at 910, having people in our home and all. There is a sense of trust – I guess that is the best word for it. And I think it comes from a sense that to move toward solidarity, to move toward this kind of political action, you have to live a *daily life* of sacrifice, and that I think is the key. And I am interested in the questions because I am *very* disturbed about the inability of white, middle-class, progressive Christians and non-Christians to *act*, and to act in a way that really brings radical social change.

Telling the history of the Imperial Hotel occupation is not about getting people to take over hotels, Eduard emphasized; it is about a witness to a way of life among the poor. That, he said, is liberation theology in a North American context.[72]

Rumination to Action

Despite the absence of expected media and police, the scene at the hotel was vibrant by mid-afternoon on the first day of the occupation. Dick Rustay remembered when Eduard came down from the top floor and exclaimed, "Open the gates! We want to invite all the homeless to

Above: Nibs Stroupe (left), Bettina Paul and Elizabeth Dede (center), Larry Travick (second from right), and John Flournoy (right), remove debris from the Imperial Hotel. Photo by Gladys Rustay, courtesy of the Open Door Community.

Right: Eduard Loring (left), John Flournoy (second from left), Phillip Williams (second from right), Carol Schlicksup (right, dark hair), and others remove debris from the Imperial Hotel. Photo by Gladys Rustay, courtesy of the Open Door Community.

stay here!" This started a whirlwind of activity for both those inside and outside the hotel.

Joe Beasley of Antioch Baptist Church North had known Eduard and Murphy through Concerned Black Clergy. He recalled that after they made the announcement to let people in, they began to clean out the old commodes, sofas, and other junk. Joe was certain this activity would bring police, but they did not arrive.

Dick recalled, "I don't know how many years the hotel had been closed, but there were lots of cans and newspapers and other things. We just pulled it out and started stacking it in the streets. As soon as that happened, people could see something going on."

This turn of events caused a disruption, something that social movement theorist Frances Fox Piven describes as "a power strategy that rests on withdrawing cooperation in social relations."[73] When the doors were opened for others to join them, and when they began getting the hotel ready for habitation, they were refusing to cooperate with accepted social norms, with normal patterns of civic life.[74]

CHAPTER FOUR
ACTION TO OCCUPATION

Elizabeth Dede described the first day as an amazing event. She recalled that many people had gathered at street level, and the activists invited them in, asking them to stay on the lower floors. Carol Schlicksup was surprised when homeless people joined them in the hotel. She was not opposed to this happening, but she later believed that the activists were not prepared for it. Nobody was certain of the intentions of some of those who entered. The protesters knew some of the homeless people, but they relied in great measure on C.M. Sherman and John Flournoy, who had both lived on the streets, to determine if a person might create problems.[75]

The protesters got an opportunity to voice their concerns late Monday afternoon as news cameras rolled. Mayor Maynard Jackson was in Chicago at the National League of Mayors meeting, but the city sent a representative. Dick Rustay distinctly remembered the exchange between the representative and Murphy when the television cameras were filming. The representative said, "You know you are letting people into a condemned building." Murphy responded, "Well isn't it terrible that it is safer to be in a condemned building than on the streets." Murphy's comment was emblazoned in Dick's mind: "It was on television, and I remember the representative's mouth sort of dropped. He was speechless." Dick considered Murphy's declaration a "powerful, powerful statement."

In an effort to get Portman to respond to the occupation, PUJ wrote a letter and sent it to him Monday evening. The letter stated:

> People for Urban Justice is a Christian social action group that
> is working for justice on behalf of the poor and homeless in the

city of Atlanta. The enclosed press packet will explain our action which began at four o'clock on Monday morning.

Now, it is seven o'clock on Monday evening and we are writing to inform you that our action is no longer symbolic. As you would have learned from your staff today, we are occupying the Imperial Hotel and will continue to do so until the city of Atlanta and its business community join together to provide affordable housing for the homeless and the poor.

Mayor Jackson has committed his administration to a policy for the homeless that provides single-room-occupancy apartments. You have bought one of the few remaining SROs, the Imperial Hotel. We have re-opened the building to show you, and Joe Martin of Central Atlanta Progress and Mayor Jackson the way to provide SROs.

Please come join us and send your construction crews to renovate the Imperial Hotel.

House the Homeless Here![76]

As the memorandum indicates, prior to the hotel occupation, Jackson made a commitment to increase the number of SROs in Atlanta. The activists were not the first to suggest that the Imperial be renovated and returned to use as an SRO. Approximately six months earlier, in a November 1989 letter to Mayor Andrew Young, Atlanta resident and scientist Charles Lee suggested that the Imperial Hotel should be re-opened as an SRO. Lee distributed food and clothes at Jesus Place, a ministry that served poor people, so he was familiar with the plight of Atlanta's poor and homeless people. He wrote:

I pass by the Imperial Hotel on Peachtree Street near Ralph McGill on a daily basis, and I have done a rough calculation that indicates more than 300 rooms that are going to waste, that could potentially be used for temporary housing for the homeless. Mayor, I understand that the property is privately owned, and that the owner (Portman, I believe) will one day raze the building to use the land for some other purpose. But, sir, could you not try to do something to possibly lease the building for renovation until the time comes for the owner to tear it down? I suggest that you could get the building repaired for only the cost of the materials and a few city people to oversee the repairs. I believe that you could obtain help from the people who might use the building to work on the repairs. In other words, allow the homeless to work at repairing the building, and let them stay in those rooms that they have repaired as they work on the others. You could even add the dignifying effect of giving them credits for their work against "rent" . . . Please consider my suggestion, or come up with a better one. It is getting cold, and we will have people who sleep in the doorways with only minimal clothing. Some will die as a result.[77]

Lee's appeal was directly to Mayor Young, and he rightly underscored that the impending winter worsened conditions for Atlanta's homeless people.

Mayor Jackson: From Progressive to Centrist

Murphy and Eduard supported some of Mayor Jackson's policies during his first two terms as mayor from 1974 to 1982. In January 1990, Murphy gave the benediction at Jackson's third-term inauguration. Murphy, Eduard, and others were hopeful that in his third term Jackson would increase efforts to make the city more hospitable to poor people. There were positive signs early in his third term that he would do that. In the months leading up to the occupation, activists had been pushing for an increase in SROs. In Eduard's March 24, 1990, letter to the *Atlanta Journal-Constitution* entitled "Housing Recognized as Solution to City Homelessness," he noted that Jackson appeared to have been interested in building more SROs. He wrote:

> I am thankful for the *Constitution*'s positive March 18 editorial "Downtown Strategy is Tough, Caring." Yes, the age of miracles continues. We have reached a point in the history of Atlanta where leaders in business, city government, and the homeless agree that the solution to homelessness is housing . . . [Mayor Jackson] called for citywide construction of single room occupancy apartments . . . Housing is the solution to homelessness. Six hundred police will not help one iota unless jobs with living wages

and benefits are available to Atlantans who are able to work (about 50 percent of the homeless), and good, affordable housing is accessible to all people. We of the homeless community estimate that the need is for 6,500 SRO units and eight non-profit and worker-owned Job Service Centers. With partnership among the homeless, business leaders, and city government, we can make Atlanta a more humane city where human needs and dignity are the bottom line and downtown is a place of joy and comfort in which to work and play.[78]

Eduard's comments point to the affordable-housing shortage while underscoring the importance of employment that pays a living wage. As he indicates in the letter, there were many homeless people who were working but could not afford a place to live. More than six thousand SRO units and eight non-profit job centers would alleviate much of the suffering that homeless people were experiencing. His closing thoughts powerfully shift the "bottom line" from financial gain and superficial status to human needs and dignity.

Even though Maynard Jackson appeared to be interested in affordable housing, by the time he took office in 1990 for his third term, he had shifted considerably from his first term, when he was fundamentally more progressive. Before assuming office in 1974 for his first term, Jackson stated that his aim was to produce "a situation whereby grass-roots leaders, white and black, will be sitting alongside of persons who are quite wealthy, quite influential, and sometimes not as attuned as they need to be to what it is really like to be living close to disaster."[79] According to political scientist Clarence Stone, for city leaders so accustomed to elite-level cooperation, "Jackson's aspiration represented a fundamental change."[80] Stone added, "Jackson likened the political and economic life of Atlanta to a table provided with food: he did not want to push anyone away; he only wanted to see that previously excluded groups could join in the feast."[81] Further, Larry Keating concluded, "Jackson's inclusive, pluralistic approach to government during his first term was a radical departure from government by an elite few, which had characterized Atlanta's politics for nearly three decades."[82]

Stone and Keating remind us that Jackson's progressive vision did not last into his second term. Stone wrote that he had mass appeal and formal power, but he "lacked command of the informal system of cooperation that was so important in the civic life of Atlanta."[83] More specifically, Stone charged:

The business elite operated with a high level of cohesion and continuity and with a daunting array of resources. Its power added up to more than the sum of its parts. Even potential rivals found it easier to move with than against the business elite, whether the goal was preserving old buildings, driving crime out of Midtown, seeking a foundation grant, or constructing nonprofit housing. Alliance with the business elite is the coalition that works – though it is an alliance that comes at the cost of acquiescence to such business interests as no city-imposed requirements on developers.[84]

Keating traces Jackson's political arc when he observes, "With Jackson at the helm, the white downtown business elite found its influence on city government diminished . . . [but] Jackson's estrangement from the business elite was neither complete nor permanent."[85] By his second term (1978), Jackson had learned about the expediency of reconciliation and capitulation, and his progressive agenda was neutered.[86]

Between Jackson's second and third term of office, Andrew Young served two terms as mayor (1982-1990). Stone summarized glaring differences between Jackson's and Young's political bent: "Whereas Maynard Jackson's alliance with the business elite was slow in coming, uneasy at best, and compromised by other constituency ties, Andrew Young's alliance was quick, firm, and unambiguous."[87] Keating suggests Young's policies were influenced by a more conservative trend in America during this period. "Young," he said, "believed that the economic development he sought was a partial antidote to black poverty and that the issues of poverty, low-income housing, and social programs were largely national and not local responsibilities." Keating added that it is also important to remember that Young was mayor during the Reagan era, and that his "pro-business stance and his reluctance to address poverty more directly reflected the conservative mood of the country during his time in office."[88] Stone suggests that in Young's administration, lower-income housing lacked priority, and even though Mayor Young was not uninterested in housing for poor people, their lack of power resulted in inattention due to competing demands."[89]

According to Charles Steffen, Jackson's return to office in 1990, after eight years of Mayor Young's "business-friendly" administration, provided housing activists "reason to hope that the city would finally awaken to the seriousness of the social crisis unfolding on the streets of downtown Atlanta."[90] They also believed that Jackson's policy goals must be backed up by action. Activists chose not to sit idly by and wait for Jackson to act on his purported efforts toward good will and cooperative engagement; rather, they viewed the transition from Young to Jackson as an opportunity to ratchet up street actions, apply pressure, and move Jackson toward tangible results in affordable housing.[91]

Settling In

The activists were surprised to find that they were still in the building at the end of the day Monday. With events unfolding in unexpected ways, the occupants had no idea how long they would remain. They realized, however, that the building was dangerous in its unkempt and dilapidated condition. As day turned into night, the participants worked together to make the building suitable for occupancy. There was no running water or electricity the first night.

By mid-evening Monday, nobody had asked the activists and homeless people to leave the hotel, so they began creating places to sleep. Robert Dobbins and Bill Watts, homeless men who had joined the activists inside the hotel, gave out buckets filled with water so people could wash themselves, and candles so people could see as the sun went down. Robert remembered that it was pitch black inside: "Everybody went to find a room, and we gave them a candle where they could help themselves up the steps. It was tough living without electricity and water, but everybody in that hotel was going to survive because we've been out on the streets. We know how to survive." The homeless people employed their knowledge and experience to help occupants who were unaccustomed to living in compromised conditions.

On the first night of the occupation, no one had blankets, sheets, or pillows. They lay down for rest, but soon discovered the place was infested with fleas and other insects, which made it difficult to sleep. Carol Schlicksup recalled: "I remember making a space to sleep." Because Carol, like everyone else, had believed that PUJ would be back at the Open Door by Monday afternoon, she had not brought anything with her such as bedding or a change of clothes. There was concern about toilets: "Of course, there were toilets, but they weren't working. I think people used those toilets that didn't work. But that's just one of those issues you've got to think about. That's something homeless people had to do anyway." After a tough battle, Mayor Jackson eventually provided portable toilets for occupants.[92]

The original activists asked people from the streets to sleep in the lobby the first night. Later, the lobby was used as a night shelter for people who needed to wake up early to go to labor pools, and when there was not enough room upstairs. The lobby also served as the location where Mercy Mobile Unit set up a sorting room for clothes and other items in later stages of the occupation. The three "Imperial Eight" members who were formerly homeless (C.M. Sherman, Larry Travick, and John Flournoy) stayed on the lower floor during the occupation.

CHAPTER FIVE

STEADFASTLY UNSETTLED
AMONG THE DEBRIS

After a fitful night for some of the occupants, on Tuesday morning, June 19, the Open Door served a breakfast of grits, eggs, coffee, and oranges to nearly 200 people at the hotel. Later that day the activists issued a press release:

> People for Urban Justice has occupied the Imperial Hotel for more than 24 hours, turning what began as a symbolic action yesterday into real housing for today. The Imperial Hotel once again is open to house the poor.
>
> More than 25 homeless people have moved into the Imperial, joining the eight PUJ members who entered the building at 4:00 a.m. Monday to re-establish its former function as a single-room-occupancy hotel – or SRO. To celebrate the Imperial's return to service, breakfast was served to about 180 people this morning. PUJ is the political arm of the Open Door Community, which prepared and served today's breakfast of grits, eggs, coffee, and oranges. The Open Door will continue to serve breakfast at the Imperial as long as this demonstration goes on.
>
> And the demonstration will go on. PUJ is committed to keeping the doors of the Imperial open until city government and the Atlanta business community can devise real solutions to the city's critical housing shortage for the poor.

Certainly the Imperial could be used for permanent housing. It is owned by John Portman, who has known great success in developing commercial and business real estate in this city. PUJ today sent a letter to Mr. Portman, encouraging him to turn his talents to renovating the Imperial Hotel, one of the few remaining [potential] SROs in Atlanta, into housing for the poor so that homeless people can come into permanent shelter. While some may argue that the building is unsafe, PUJ would like to point out that it is far more secure than living on the streets.

The people who have moved into the Imperial in the last 24 hours – including one mother with her two small children – already have started the clean-up process. The residents are cleaning out one room at a time and as each newcomer moves in, he or she joins the forces carting out debris and sweeping out broken glass. More people continue to move in all the time, a sure indication of the crying need for housing.

While PUJ celebrates the return of the Imperial to service as an SRO, the need does not stop here. Few SROs have been built recently while many have been closed. Only 130 units have been added in recent years while this city needs 5,000. PUJ also objects to the recent closing of the city's West Hunter [Street Baptist Church] Shelter and the anticipated closing of the Rising Star Shelter.[93] But instead of addressing this pressing and growing need, the city and business community have elected to devote their energies to sports and entertainment projects, including the Olympics, Super Bowl, and Underground Atlanta, to name a few.

People for Urban Justice would like to remind Mayor Maynard Jackson that his administration has promised to provide single-room-occupancy apartments, a promise on which he has not yet delivered. PUJ has re-opened the Imperial to show Mayor Jackson, Joe Martin of Central Atlanta Progress, and Mr. Portman the way to provide SROs.[94]

The press release broadcast the urgent need for affordable housing, and the activists finally began getting attention. That same day, the *Atlanta*

Constitution published a story about the occupation. The story, "Protesters Take Over Vacant Historic Property Downtown" briefly described what had transpired over the initial 24 hours of the occupation: "Without a bill of sale or a rent slip, eight protesters entered an abandoned historic downtown hotel Monday and claimed it as a new shelter for the homeless. They even began cleaning and making breakfast plans for the new tenants they invited." The writer captured Eduard's comments:

> We're here to say there are plenty of buildings in Atlanta. This is one of them, and we're going to invite people here to live and work . . . The empty shell of the Imperial is visual testimony to [John Portman's] and the business communities' indifference to the critical shortage of affordable housing for the homeless and the poor . . . This indifference is shared by a city government that has been more intent on promoting Atlanta's national and international image.[95]

By this time, Portman's employees had asked the protesters to leave the building. Portman spokesperson Danielle Martin said, "We have asked them to leave . . . We're going to see if they respond to our request. We will certainly give them time to think about alternatives and remove themselves peacefully." She added that her company considered the building unsafe for habitation, having been vacant for the last ten years. But Martin noted that Portman Holdings, Portman's development firm, had no immediate plans for the property.[96]

The Atlanta press, finally engaged, began to give the protest exposure. On Wednesday, June 20, the *Gwinnett Daily News* printed a story entitled "Prettiest Room in Town":

> The accommodations seemed as splendid as they once had been to about 70 of Atlanta's homeless who had drifted in after word spread that there was a safe and clean place to spend the night. The fact that the owner of the property, noted developer John Portman, didn't want them there seemed of little concern. Compared to the culverts, abandoned sheds, hospital waiting rooms, and alleys where many of them are accustomed to spending nights, the old and derelict hostelry was comfort and security. "I feel good," said Bobby Jones, a short, heavy-set woman who had spent the night

with her two daughters, Patches, 10, and Mary, 8, "at the Grady's" – the waiting room at Grady Hospital. "We went to a church on Butler Street, and they told us to come here for breakfast. I helped clean up as much as I could. I had a bath. I feel good."[97]

The story continued:

The main lobby and adjoining rooms were in fact cleaner than they had been in at least ten years, when the last of a handful of single-room occupancy residents were routed out and the building abandoned. As the seekers of shelter and food drifted in Tuesday, they were put to work scrubbing walls, hauling out mounds of debris and filth to be piled on the sidewalks, even cleaning the once-plush old carpets and painting crusty wooden molding. By nightfall, the premises – lit by portable electric generators – were more habitable than the living spaces many of them were accustomed to. The anterooms of what once was the Moulin Rouge Lounge – where strippers wallowed in giant champagne glasses to the delight of out-of-town businessmen – were spread with mats and blankets for sleeping. Some places were reserved for women, others for men. Some were blanketed off for two or three couples. Cardboard No Smoking signs were hung throughout the lobby.

Homeless people appreciated having a safe, comfortable place to sleep:

"It beats the hell out of sleeping under the bridge," said a burly young blond man wearing a khaki fatigue jacket in the 94-degree weather. One of the couples, Lauren Cooper of Chicago and Steve Moore of New York, whose regular habitat has been an abandoned MARTA shed off Courtland Street, had succeeded nicely in sprucing up a blanketed-off back room. Beneath the maze of gold and green wallpaper and on top of mauve-colored carpet they had assembled a packing crate bed covered with blankets. Their few belongings were neatly stacked against a wall. "It's the prettiest room in town," beamed Cooper.[98]

The story also indicated the activists' resolve to stay in the building:

A spokesman for Mayor Maynard Jackson, who has made some dramatic moves toward solving the [low-income housing] problem this spring, told the group Monday that the mayor promises a space for 200 homeless persons within 10 days. The squatters said they would believe it when they see it. Representatives of the Portman organization had warned them during the day that they could not stay, citing reasons of safety in the dilapidated old structure.[99]

C.M. Sherman's statements in the story were particularly powerful:

"They don't seem to be too worried about the safety of these people when they're sleeping on the streets or under bridges," scoffed C.M. Sherman, a resident at Open Door for three years and a partner in the non-profit organization. "We think it's a bunch of baloney." Atlanta police said they could not remove the interlopers without a formal complaint from Portman. By late Tuesday, none had been made. "It doesn't matter," said Sherman. "We'll be here as long as they'll let us. They'll have to carry us out. But our plan is to stay here until we can walk out and go to decent housing."

The activists vowed that if they were forcibly removed from the hotel, they would continue occupying buildings until the city did something to provide affordable housing. "If they kick us out, we'll just take over another one . . . There are buildings like this all over Atlanta," said a 35-year-old unemployed bookkeeper."[100]

The press also reported that the Open Door served meals at the hotel while occupants made it habitable, and that the occupation did not adversely affect office workers nearby, whose routines continued largely uninterrupted:

Meanwhile, much of the daily operation of the Open Door on Ponce [de Leon], where hundreds of homeless are fed daily, had been moved to the hotel foyer. [C.M.] Sherman said about 200 received breakfast there Tuesday. While rows of men and a handful of women continued their unauthorized cleaning operation or lounged on a brick wall inside the cool, dark lobby of the old hotel, scores of well-turned-out office workers began to emerge from the tall buildings nearby. BMWs and Audis and Mercedes snaked from the Imperial Hotel parking lot, now fenced off and commercialized, past the seedy bustle. The young men in white shirts, long sleeves buttoned at the wrist, ties drawn tight in the stifling five o'clock heat, and the coiffured women in their air-conditioned cars appeared not to, or chose not to, notice the sharp edge of contrast.[101]

The Open Door moved their Butler Street Breakfast to the Imperial Hotel during the occupation. Open Door residents, PUJ activists, and other volunteers transported tables to the Imperial and set them up in front; people formed a line to get a hot breakfast of grits, sausage, and coffee. And the breakfast began drawing more people to the occupation.

By Wednesday, June 20, more than 70 homeless people had taken up residence in the hotel. Occupants had cleared out rubbish and a large pile of debris had been placed on Ralph McGill Boulevard, which was closed to traffic and had been deeded to Portman as part of his development of One Peachtree Center, a 60-story office tower that was scheduled to open in 1992. PUJ released another press release on Wednesday:

> People for Urban Justice and as many as 75 homeless people have now occupied the former Imperial Hotel for more than two days. We have been busy cleaning and painting the first floor and have renamed the hotel "Welcome Home." Because our numbers have grown so significantly we now must move to the second floor and begin to clean it out. There is a large pile of debris already on Peachtree Center Street, and the city sanitation department has asked John Portman and Associates, Inc. to remove this pile. The inhabitants of Welcome Home will eat breakfast with an estimated 200 homeless people at six thirty on Wednesday morning and begin to clean out the second floor. We will by necessity add debris to the already large pile, resulting most likely in an obstruction of traffic. The inhabitants of Welcome Home wish to be responsible citizens. We are attempting to live in a cleaner, safer environment. Therefore, we call on Mr. Portman to see to it that the debris is removed and the street cleared. Alternatively, Mr. Portman could sign over clear title of the former Imperial Hotel to the homeless

people of Atlanta, who are residing there. We would then happily have the debris removed.[102]

The name "Welcome Home" (later changed to "Welcome House") signified the hospitality they were offering to Atlanta's homeless people; it was also a pointed reference to Maynard Jackson's return that day to Atlanta from a trip to Chicago.

The city refused to clean up the pile of debris and ordered Portman Properties to clean it up. Around 11:00 a.m. a Portman bulldozer with a scoop arrived and lifted the trash into a large trailer while hotel occupants cheered. By late afternoon another trailer was brought in to haul away the debris.[103] As the occupation continued, it seemed that the Imperial Hotel had developed into a headache for Portman. He was already constrained from including the Imperial in any massive development project because it and the building adjacent to it, Sacred Heart Catholic Church, were included on the National Historic Registry.[104] Both buildings were protected from demolition, and now the Imperial was occupied by activists whom he was reluctant to remove.

On Wednesday, Jackson met with Portman at Portman and Associates offices in downtown Atlanta. Neither Portman nor Jackson wanted the negative publicity that would likely be associated with removing the occupants. Portman had not filed a complaint with the police.[105] Without a formal complaint, the police were powerless to interfere.

After his meeting with Portman, Jackson went to the Imperial Hotel, just a few blocks away, arriving late in the afternoon. He met with the occupants

Ed Potts, Jay Frazier, and Ike Carmack serve breakfast at the Imperial Hotel during the occupation. Photo by Gladys Rustay, courtesy of the Open Door Community.

and they led him through the building. During the tour, Jackson solemnly walked along the dark hallways as the occupants sang, chanted, and clapped. He looked into rooms that had been cleared of trash, scrubbed clean, and outfitted with blankets, beds, and makeshift furniture. After touring the building he said, "This place is a disaster waiting to happen, a firetrap . . . You're here at your own risk."[106] Murphy Davis answered him: "Homelessness is a disaster and it's not waiting to happen. How can you say that living in this building is more unsafe than life on the streets?"

Frances ("Mother PUJ") Pauley with 8-year-old Mary Cox. Mary stayed inside the hotel with her 10-year-old sister Patches and her mother, Bobby Cox Jones, during the occupation. Photo by Murphy Davis, courtesy of the Open Door Community.

As he made his way through the hotel, Mayor Jackson implored the occupants to work with him as he sought affordable housing. Amid the cheers and applause, he said, "Work with me. I'm with you. I don't want to live in a city where you don't have decent housing."[107] But, he cautioned, the city could not do it alone. Jackson promised the occupants that a new shelter with a capacity of 260 people would open July 2. Since his arrival at Hartsfield Airport earlier in the day, in fact, he had gotten a commitment from local architects to provide a plan for construction of SROs. He gave his word that he would "throw his weight" behind the project.[108] C.M. Sherman asked the mayor, "Can you promise we will have a place to sleep if we leave here?" Jackson said he could not promise that.[109] Laura Cooper, who had been homeless for two years, asked, "May we stay here, permanently?" Jackson responded, "I don't own this building, I can't give it to you."[110] Jackson's words were unsatisfactory: occupants wanted permanent, affordable housing.

Although Jackson and Portman did not want to remove the hotel occupants by force, there *were* efforts to lure them out of the building. The day after Jackson's tour of the hotel on June 20, city building inspectors declared the building unsafe.[111] This declaration spurred Jackson to attempt to empty the building under the guise of safety concerns. Citing potential hazards in the dilapidated building, Jackson and other officials urged everyone to leave.

Reporters gather at the Imperial Hotel. Photo courtesy of the Open Door Community.

Joe Beasley acknowledged that the building was unsafe, but thought it best that folks remain inside: "Of course you could look at it and tell that it really was not a safe building, but it was safer, in our view, than people sleeping out in cat holes and so forth. It had been sitting there for years and hadn't burned down, and we felt comfort that the Lord was with us."

Jackson received approval to open a temporary shelter at Grady High School, but this did not appease the hotel occupants. The city had set up 200 cots, and the school had functioning bathrooms and showers. Aaron Turpeau, Jackson's chief of staff, urged the squatters to abandon the hotel for the safety and comfort of the school. They spurned his offer, indicating they wanted permanent housing. Bill Jones, a leader of the homeless contingent inside the hotel, exclaimed, "I want to stay right here. We don't want your shelter. We want housing." The others chanted, "We want housing."[112]

Only six people showed up at Grady High. Like city-run shelters, it was planned that Grady High would not serve food, and residents were required to vacate the building from 7:00 a.m. to 6:00 p.m. It would remain open for roughly three weeks, until the expected opening of a new shelter at 234 Memorial Drive.[113]

Murphy Davis remembered Aaron Turpeau entering the hotel and announcing the offer of shelter at Grady High: "He came into the front hallway of the hotel, which was jammed with advocates and homeless people. There were hot, sweaty bodies packed together and bursting with hope and empowerment. When Aaron offered the school gym for shelter he was shouted down and unable to say another word. He finally sheepishly squirmed out of the hotel and never returned."

The hotel occupants did not want temporary shelter: they sought affordable housing. The occupants insisted that shelters offered little safety, no privacy, and restricted freedom. The *Orlando Sentinel* reported:

> "We don't want shelters. We want housing – single-room-occupancy housing for all the homeless," said Laura Cooper, 34, who had been sleeping in an empty mass-transit warehouse before moving Tuesday to the Imperial. Although city inspectors say the derelict hotel is unsafe for habitation, Cooper considers it less dangerous than sleeping in parks or shelters. "I feel safer here than on the street," Cooper said, her left arm bandaged where she had been stabbed with a broken beer bottle. "This is my little domain. It's not much, but it's shelter. It's home." Her bed is a door covered with a couple of blankets. A square piece of foam rubber serves as a pillow. Beside her bed are possessions: a flashlight, a transistor radio, a candle and a rose. For privacy she has tacked a yellow blanket over the doorway and placed a piece of cardboard in front of a window with broken glass and burglar bars. Her toilet is a coffee can.[114]

Ten-year-old Patches Cox and her 34-year-old mother, Bobby Cox Jones, and 8-year-old sister, Mary Cox had most recently been living in an apartment near Perry Homes housing project. Even though the hotel was in rough condition, Patches said that she felt safer there than in her former apartment.[115]

The occupants did not know how long they would be in the hotel, but knew that it would not be forever, Robert Dobbins claimed. A rumor circulated that Portman had said he would burn down the hotel before he would let the occupants remain in it. On Thursday, June 21, the *Gwinnett Daily News* reported that Mayor Jackson convinced Portman not to forcefully remove the occupants until July 2 (the day the new shelter was scheduled to open).[116] PUJ was unaware of this proposed date. Carol Schlicksup noted that PUJ wanted to negotiate with the city so that the homeless people were not forced back onto the street. She said, "We were eventually going back to the Open Door to sleep in beds, and we didn't want the homeless people back on the street."

Eduard Loring and Elizabeth Dede talk to reporter Ben Smith III from within the Imperial Hotel. Photo courtesy of the Open Door Community.

Joe Beasley did not recall that PUJ and the homeless occupants were asked to leave by a specific date, but he remarked that the discussions indicated who held the reins of power: "Whoever pays the piper calls the tune." This, he said, is capitalism overlaid with so-called democracy: "The mayor, who is a part of the democratic process, has to get elected, and if you're going to get elected then that means you've got to get some money to run a campaign, and since the people who have the money to sponsor the campaign are the capitalists like Portman, then Portman was calling a lot of the shots." Joe believed that PUJ was a powerful group, at least on a symbolic level, and that, given their visibility, it would not be "good politics" to lock them up.

Occupants recalled that Portman was never seen at the hotel during the occupation. He remained deliberately in the background while city officials were left to cope with the occupation. This likely means that Portman either relinquished power to Jackson at their Wednesday, June 20, meeting, or perhaps more astutely from Portman's perspective, he handed over a political quagmire to Jackson. Either way, it is clear that Jackson managed the occupation, not Portman.

Portman's distance was felt immediately. Carol Schlicksup pointed out that on the first day of the occupation, though Portman's security staff and Atlanta police officers knew PUJ was in the hotel, they did not do anything to remove them. "They cruised by," Carol said, and "maybe some stopped by to talk to some of the folks on the Executive Committee or to Eduard and C.M., but I don't remember that they asked us to leave."

Supporters of the Imperial action carry a banner near the Imperial Hotel. Photo courtesy of the Open Door Community.

Eduard asserted, "Of course Portman didn't visit the hotel during the occupation: he was too rich and powerful to be 'visible' to the poor and the agitators."

The occupation became a problem for the city and not for Portman. "At the time I felt like he had Jackson over a barrel," Carol stated. "It became a city issue, but the city didn't own the hotel, and there was only so much the city could do."

Portman would have had to press trespassing charges to get the occupants evicted. "Can you imagine?" Carol asked. "Arresting these folks for criminal trespass – people who are poor and without any place to stay. So maybe Jackson also thought that would be a mistake for the city. Maybe it was an agreement they had, politically between the two of them, and Jackson said, 'I'll handle it' – maybe that's more of the deal."[117]

On the 24th, the *Orlando Sentinel* published a story entitled "Defiant Check-In at Imperial Hotel: 200 Squatters find No-Cost Housing." They summarized the week's events:

> The Imperial Hotel is anything but regal. The 80-year-old structure's glory days are long gone. Even its ignoble tenure as a flophouse ended a decade ago. But like some beacon of bleakness, the old hotel of red brick and bay windows is once again drawing people to its vacant rooms. A group of homeless squatters, growing larger every day, has hijacked the hotel in defiance of the city's most influential developer and its most powerful politician. Neither John Portman, who is building a $445 million office tower and merchandise mart next door, nor

Mayor Maynard Jackson has been able to persuade the squatters to leave the building.[118]

At the end of the first week, the activists had been joined by more than 200 people from the street. The article reported: "The group has placed banners and placards outside the Imperial's entrance, protesting the lack of low-income housing at a time when the city is spending millions of dollars on Underground Atlanta, the Georgia Dome stadium, and bids to host a Super Bowl and the 1996 Olympics."

Even though they were settling in, the occupiers remained unsettled. They continued to raise their voices inside the hotel and outside on the streets.

CHAPTER SIX

HOSPITALITY IN A BEACON OF BLEAKNESS

Central to daily life at the hotel were efforts to make it habitable and hospitable. Occupants worked to clean it and make others welcome. Robert Dobbins, a homeless man staying at the hotel, recalled that there were about 90 people a day at the hotel – and even more when it rained. The occupants worked together to make the hotel a safer and more comfortable place: "We swept out the rooms, but we couldn't afford to paint 'em up and put up new sheet rock." Some of the occupants left the hotel to work during the day. Those who did not, labored to improve the living conditions of the hotel. Robert recalled there was no "just comin' in layin' around, there was none of that."

Robert slept on a blanket and said that some people brought their own bedding and that local churches delivered mats for people to use. At night, women and men stayed in different areas of the building and children slept with their mothers. The occupants were running the place as if it were a hotel again. Newcomers were registered and then assigned a room. Inside the hotel there was a buzz of activity; outside, media attention flourished.

Despite sleeping on cardboard spread over a tattered box spring, 46-year-old Phillip Stewart was happy to have a home. He was also proud that he had worked 18-hour days for the past week, cleaning out debris in the building. A former hotel custodian, Stewart had recently lost his job and apartment; he now found himself "on the front line of the most militant action ever taken on behalf of homeless people in Atlanta."[119] Kenneth Charles Walker, a thirty-five-year-old unemployed, homeless carpenter, observed, "I had quit. I had given up. I was convinced that no one gave a damn about anything but themselves. But this group has brought purpose back to me."[120]

The *Atlanta Journal-Constitution* continued to cover the story, telling its readers that the occupants had reached a point where there was no turning back. They quoted Eduard: "We believe it's a crime the city can find money for Underground, and the dome, and the Olympics, but has done virtually nothing for those who have no place to sleep at night. We simply can't wait any longer for empty promises."[121]

The *Revolutionary Worker* carried this statement by an unnamed homeless man: "A lot of shelters got closed for the summer, and there's no place for the homeless to stay. There's a lot of us here – 14,000 in the city of Atlanta. It's dangerous in the streets. So basically [People for] Urban Justice came and made a home for us here at the hotel. A lot of us can't afford housing. We can't afford rent, and a lot of us just want a safe place to stay. We're not safe in the streets. We can't sleep in the park or we'll go to jail." He added, "I know guys that are going to jail just so that they can get off the streets, to have a place to stay and something to eat! . . . You got a lot of brothers and sisters out here with a lot of skills. You've got professional bricklayers, professional plumbers and electricians. But when they talk about us, all they see is dope monsters, alcoholics, robbers, burglars – they're all putting us here in a category. But we are all human beings." He was tired of broken promises: "Everything is always, 'We're gonna build this for you,' or 'We're gonna get this for you,' 'We're gonna bring this many people in later down the road; we're gonna have this many jobs.' This is the one time that people got together and just said 'fuck it!' We're gonna do this now, this is for the here and now."[122]

John Scruggs at the Open Door Community, 2005. Photo by author.

John Scruggs was homeless in Atlanta during the occupation. He described the scene when he entered the hotel: "I basically was cold that evening and I was walkin' down the street and I saw one of my friends and he said, 'We can go in here man, and lay down.'"[123] Scruggs was worn out from the streets. Someone offered him a bologna sandwich, and a woman gave him one of her blankets. John appreciated these acts of hospitality, especially considering the circumstances: "It warmed my heart to find out what was going on."

A welcoming environment permeated the hotel during the occupation. John had learned to survive on Atlanta's streets after he lost his job in Tucker, Georgia, and his knowledge, skill, and compassion enabled others inside the hotel to be more comfortable. He recalled:

> After I lost my job I came down here to Atlanta. That's when I got involved in learning how to survive the street. You see, these people already had this stuff goin', which was new to me because this was my first time being homeless. I didn't know anything about that, so what I had to get involved in was how to survive, how to get with the people who were already homeless and how to survive, where to go to get you something to eat, how many days I got to wear my socks and underwear before I take a bath, how to take off a shirt and let somebody else wear it when they're cold, and if I got an extra blanket then give it to somebody. I had to learn how to do this. When you're out on the street and homeless you've got to share with everybody because they're going to share with you. That's the code. I had to learn about that.

PUJ members continued to deal with matters as they arose, and kept a positive attitude. Carol Schlicksup said, "There were issues that needed to be dealt with, but for the most part it was a positive feeling. The atmosphere was one of expectation and excitement."

One of the overriding issues was safety. "There were so many people joining us and we wanted to keep everybody safe and to know who was there because perhaps not everybody was there for the same reason," Carol emphasized. Despite concerns, Carol believed that people inside the hotel remained in positive spirits: "The thought was that we were doing what we could. And, in fact, something would come of this, and it did – not as quickly as I had hoped, but it did come eventually."

Carol estimated that there were approximately three hundred people in and around the hotel at different points during the occupation. Jo Ann Geary felt that it was a blessing that so many different organizations, churches, and individuals brought supplies such as food and bottled water. Sometimes they donated money. Further, she appreciated that people dropped in just to check on them to see how they were doing, and to make sure that they were safe. Jo Ann remembered that she was inspired by the women in the hotel:

> To walk down a hall and to see their faces, and to see how nicely they kept their rooms, how they cleaned them up and had a little table, how they were making it home. They had a place and they felt safe. I remember how good that made me feel – that they felt safe because you can talk about the streets and you can talk about how we have all these shelters, but most shelters are not safe, they're wall-to-wall people, and they are not treated like human beings.

An Operation in Motion

Individual and group acts of kindness at the Imperial mirrored the kind of hospitality offered at the Open Door Community. At the time of the occupation, the Open Door was regularly serving lunch and breakfast to homeless and indigent people. Breakfast was served at Butler Street CME Church. Dick and Gladys Rustay and the twenty or so others who remained at the Open Door struggled to meet the demands the occupation created.

Dick recalled, "We would bring food from the Open Door for lunch to try to feed the people in there. We were scrambling right and left. We

Laura Cooper, a leader during the occupation, works out details. Photo courtesy of the Open Door Community.

were improvising." None of the activists had a cell phone, and one of the difficulties house residents faced was communication with the hotel occupants. Dick recalled, "They'd suddenly call and want something, or ask 'Where is it?' and we'd say, 'Where is what?' . . . The hall phone at the Open Door was very, very busy."

One strategy that had been used at the Open Door to keep order and serve the needs of Atlanta's homeless people was to keep a schedule so everyone in the house knew what their assignments were for the coming week. This schedule was usually created by a leader in the house. During the occupation, the list was altered: instead of a leader assigning duties, Dick and Gladys posted a sign-up sheet on the wall and people filled in their names next to a job. "It was out of kilter," Dick remarked. Tensions flared at times. Dick said, "I remember that people would be angry and we didn't know quite why, and it was just the lack of communication." One of the biggest problems was trying to meet the occupants' needs and figuring out how to get those items to the hotel and still maintain what they were doing at the house.

Some of the Open Door residents would go to the hotel for the day to support the occupants. Sometimes they would stay there all night. At that time people were allowed to sleep in the yard at the Open Door, and so there was a large number of people in and around the house requiring attention, and this created tension. Gladys and Dick were fairly new to the house, and they were thrust into a leadership position that they had not expected and did not feel entirely comfortable with. Immediately after the action started getting press coverage, people began dropping off food and other supplies at the Imperial, removing some of the pressure from Open Door residents to fulfill all of the occupants' needs. People inside the hotel were delighted that they received this kind of assistance.

Looking back at this hectic time, Dick relayed, "I know there were lots of times we were ready to pull our hair out, and we just reflected afterwards how important it was to set up communications systems. It wasn't as good as it could have been. We didn't know each other as well. And people were just improvising. The hotel occupants were always wanting ice water or extra food or things like that, so we'd have to try to get it to them."

Dick clearly recalled serving breakfast at the hotel: "Back then we served oranges instead of orange juice, and we cooked grits in three pots – that's all our stove could take. We got there at 7:00 a.m., and set up right in front, right next to the huge trash pile that was 15 or 20 feet tall." This location put the activists in a visible location where all passersby could see them.

Dick was quick to point out that even though there was tension and frustration at the house, "it was just an amazing time, and there were almost twenty people trying to maintain the soup kitchen and the breakfast." The occupation, however, translated to more hungry bellies that needed to be fed. Open Door residents delivered sandwiches and drinks to the hotel occupants. "They always had a long list of needs," Dick recalled. The Open Door had only one van during the occupation, which was put to hard use.

Dick stated that he and Gladys were still "feeling their way" at the time of the occupation, still acclimating to the Open Door after only eight months of living there. They had to take full responsibility for the house, and it took them a while to figure out how to manage the situation.

"There's always layer after layer of realizing what it takes to run the place," Dick said. "It was a matter of trying to keep the house going." Looking back, Dick better understood why they faced such difficulty in the house: "It's always difficult to have two things at once. Usually we just try to focus on one thing. Whenever we don't do that, it's always difficult to survive." Dick remarked, "I know with most street actions, we try to just focus on the action. And that was the intent, but it turned out to be something different . . . I think everyone was supportive of it, but we didn't have the wherewithal to get things done as well as we could have."

When Eduard pondered how much Dick and Gladys accomplished at the Open Door during the occupation, it confirmed his belief that they were (and still are) "heroes and servants." Dick, Gladys, and other Open Door residents and volunteers worked cooperatively to bring comfort to the hotel occupants. This reminded Eduard of the way Jesus and his disciples did not need seminary training to practice hospitality: "All they needed was the streets and a hunger for justice."

CHAPTER SEVEN
SINGING OUT FOR JUSTICE

A s occupants settled into the hotel, music became a vital part of the action. Music has always been part of the Open Door Community. Murphy Davis is an accomplished guitarist and vocalist who, for many years, has led singing at Open Door events and street actions. PUJ used music in their actions to unite people for a common cause. During the occupation, music served as a source and sign of strength, solidarity, and commitment. As it had done in the civil rights movement thirty years earlier, music helped build bridges across generations, among people of different races and classes, and between leaders and followers, which helped reinforce the notion that everyone belonged to the same Beloved Community.[124]

"Open Door always sings," Robert Dobbins declared. Robert was part of the hotel occupation and he explained the power of singing: "Time seemed to go by better in them days. Spirituals help the time go by better because you're takin' your mind off your situation and puttin' it in another. It's just like it could be freezin' cold out there but if you don't think about it you're gonna be warm. You put God first." For Robert, singing and music connected him to God by comforting him in the present and giving him hope for the future: "It had to be religious beliefs that helped you get through it. You had to have hope come from somewhere, you know."

Internationally renowned artist and Atlanta resident Elise Witt led singing during the hotel occupation.[125] Witt, who for many years has shared music and song at the Open Door, described an important distinction between *performing* and *leading* music: "Singing at the Imperial was not about playing something FOR people – yes, listening to music can uplift us – but

Murphy Davis plays guitar and sings at worship while Houston Wheeler (center), Jim Milner (second from right), and others participate during the Imperial Hotel occupation. Photo courtesy of the Open Door Community.

it's getting people singing communally that has the power to move us. So if you're occupying, it's long and it's not romantic and it's hours and days and weeks and months, and to band together and sing together revs up the motors again and again and brings everybody together."

James West Davidson and Michael Stoff reveal some of the roots of movement music when they write: "Songs have always moved people to action. They provided courage to Christian martyrs consumed by the fires of persecution, boldness to the French revolutionaries who marched on the Bastille, and defiant comfort to Jews bound for Nazi crematoria."[126] In the United States, the 19th- and 20th-century populist movements, the civil rights movement, and other types of justice actions used music and song to unite supporters for a common cause. More recently, the Occupy movement harnessed music and song to express outrage about the housing crisis.

Homeless hotel occupant Stanley Gibson remembered that during the takeover participants sang "old African American spirituals." The songs motivated Stanley; they gave him strength and stamina and faith that things were going to work out. He recalled that many people sang, and it was loud and the songs rang out. For Stanley, singing during the occupation heightened the spiritual awareness and the seriousness of the purpose: "I felt a sense of accomplishment that things were going to work and that there was nothin' that could break this thing down. They say strength comes in numbers and I really felt it."

Cultural critics Ron Eyerman and Andrew Jamison suggest that an integral component of music in social movements is how it *mobilizes tradition* (using old songs for new purposes) toward a collective consciousness. They argue that "through its ritualized performance and through the memories it invokes, the music of social movements transcends the boundaries of the self and binds the individual to a collective consciousness."[127] Here, they say, is where "individual and collective identity fuse and where past and future are reconnected to the present in a meaningful way."[128] Their ideas suggest that when people are singing for a common goal, music and song encourage them to move beyond a less powerful singular perspective toward a more powerful collective perspective.

According to sociologist Frances Fox Piven, shared music and song can form a repertoire for a language of resistance.[129] Singing in unison can foster "a common commitment to work for social and political change."[130] Even though it remains a mystery exactly *how* music and song move people for a common cause, Davidson and Stoff observe that it is no mystery how folk artist Pete Seeger moved his listeners while uniting them for a larger goal:

> He understood that listening was not enough. He invited audiences to sing along, so that each voice joined with others, building to an emotion-filled climax and binding people together. His "hootenannies" transformed passive listeners into full-throated actors, no longer an audience but now a part of the medium *and* the message. In the process, Seeger turned the performer's "I" into a chorus of "we" with an enormous potential. Put another way, the physical act of singing together creates an imagined sense of community and involvement, the musical analogue of

"participatory democracy" that can drive action beyond the stage, the concert, and the music hall.[131]

The mobilization of tradition reached its zenith in the United States in the 1950s and 1960s during the civil rights movement. Spirituals, hymns, and slave songs became useful cultural material during the struggle for civil rights. In her memoir, *Freedom Song*, Mary King, a member of the Student Non-Violent Coordinating Committee, writes that "the repertoire of 'freedom songs' [sung at demonstrations] had an unparalleled ability to evoke the moral power of the movement's goals, to arouse the spirit, comfort the afflicted, instill courage and commitment, and to unite disparate strangers into a 'band of brothers and sisters' and a 'circle of trust.'"[132]

During the Imperial occupation, music and song provided expression, bonding, and hope for the activists. Occupants sang "We Shall Not be Moved" as Mayor Jackson toured the hotel on the third day of the takeover.[133] Other songs included "This Little Light of Mine," "I'm on My Way," and "I've Got a Building," a tune from Ghana that Murphy had learned from Rev. Ron Spann of Detroit ("I've got a building, never made by hand . . . This is the building of justice . . . Never made by hand . . . This is the building of freedom . . . never made by hand . . .").

"We Shall Overcome" was a constant refrain inside the building and outside on the sidewalk. This song, of course, became *the* anthem of the civil rights movement, and it has been used around the world to unite people in struggles for justice. The lyrics are unadorned yet powerful: "We shall overcome, we shall overcome / We shall overcome some day / Deep in my heart, I do believe / We shall overcome some day." Other verses evoke a similar, equally simple message: "We'll walk hand in hand / We shall live in peace." Scholar Allan Winkler writes that the power of this song lies in its "quiet simplicity that reflected the passion of activists' commitment to social justice and the strength of their resolve to bring about social change."[134]

The transformation of "We Shall Overcome" from an old spiritual song into the anthem of the civil rights movement is instructive in terms of how songs can mobilize tradition and perform cultural work. Winkler details the transformation:

> In 1946, while working as the music director at Highlander [Center], Zilphia Horton heard striking black tobacco workers

singing to keep up their spirits. Their song was 'We Will Overcome,' based loosely on an old spiritual called 'I'll Be All Right.' Sung very slowly, it became her favorite song. [Pete] Seeger learned it from her in 1947 and published it in People's Songs that year. He sped up the tempo, singing it with a banjo rhythm, and made a significant change. "We Will Overcome" became "We Shall Overcome."[135]

Seeger changed the word "Will" to "Shall" for musical reasons. He said: "I think I liked a more open sound; 'We will' has alliteration to it, but 'We shall' opens the mouth wider; the 'i' in 'will' is not an easy vowel to sing well."[136] More important, perhaps, is that in the transformation from "I'll be alright" to "We shall overcome," the "collective noun replaced the singular, reflecting a shift in the locus of redemption, from sacred to secular, or at least from the individual to the group."[137] The dignified locution of the song, and perhaps the physical gestures involved in groups of people joining hands

Police and others at the Imperial Hotel during the occupation. Photo courtesy of the Open Door Community.

when they sang it, impressed Martin Luther King Jr. After hearing Seeger sing the song in 1957, King observed, "That song really sticks with you, doesn't it?"[138]

Elise Witt believes that music and singing can radically alter the atmosphere of an event. She suggested that singing vibrates our bodies and changes the surrounding space in palpable ways: "It can completely change our molecules; it changes our temperament. Music is extremely powerful in that way." She recalled how Bernice Johnson Reagon, founder of Sweet Honey in the Rock (and historian, composer, and activist), in an interview with Bill Moyers, articulated that during the civil rights movement people were gathered in churches and they knew that the police were coming with dogs and it was a dangerous situation. Reagon explained that the people inside the churches began singing and it would change the air around them. Witt added, "I've never forgotten that, and I feel that every time that I sing with groups; it is what is most powerful for me."

In addition to leading songs at the Imperial Hotel, Witt drew upon another strategy to get people to sing together: zipper songs. Folk artist and labor activist Lee Hays, a member of The Weavers in the 1950s, coined the term "zipper song" to describe how writers would compose simple songs with repeating verses so that "you have to zip in only a word or two to make an entirely new verse."[139] Hays penned labor songs by revising hymns he had learned in his youth at religious camps in Arkansas. The power of a zipper song lies in its malleability, the way that "you can zip out one word or phrase and zip in something that's appropriate to the situation you are singing about," explained Witt. For example, with a song like "This Little Light of Mine," Witt could lead a group to sing the main verse "This little light of mine, I'm gonna let it shine," and then follow it with: "All around the Imperial Hotel, I'm gonna let it shine; All across Atlanta, I'm gonna let it shine; All across the USA, I'm gonna let it shine; All around the world, I'm gonna let it shine; Deep in my heart, I'm gonna let it shine."

By adding verses to fit particular situations, songs perform cultural work. After all, Witt observed, when songs are released from their role as entertainment, they can perform their "job" as tools for collaboration and community building. Witt declared: "You have to have songs that get better and better, that get more thrilling and exciting and wonderful as you sing them, and you start zipping out something and zipping in something else, and somebody can just call out the next verse, and it keeps on building. It really is this big communal process."

Witt understands that group participation is a vital component of justice struggles. She said, for example, that the songs that invite participation are those that have repeated refrains and "simple repetitive choruses and rhyming couplets, with an emotional and political content."[140] Witt described these kinds of songs as deceptively simple. "They are actually very complex and very deep," she said, "but we have some of that knowledge in our collective memory and in our culture growing up, and there are certain songs that you can teach and people get them right away, because the way that they are made, the construction of the songs are so deep in our collective memory, and there's a lot of repetition (in words but also in melodies) so that they go where we expect them to, and they feel good to sing." Ultimately, Witt and other song leaders at the Imperial Hotel created accessible "movement" music that sought "transcendence through common struggle" while evoking belief in "possibility, hope, and change."[141]

Calvin Kimbrough, a pastor, partner, and resident at the Open Door Community continues the tradition of music-making at the Open Door. As co-coordinator of art and music (with his wife Nelia, also a pastor, partner, and resident), Calvin draws from a deep well of spiritual, labor, and folk songs when leading music at Sunday Worship, during political actions, and at Open Door special events such as holiday meals for people living on the streets. Primarily trained as a documentary photographer and filmmaker, and interested in recording events that present an alternative to the status quo, Calvin uses his guitar or banjo to produce rhythm-driven songs with percussive timbre that evoke, ideally, both consciousness-raising and communal participation. "The chief thing that I am after is having people sing together," he said, and added, "I feel that my primary tool to achieve that is rhythm."[142]

Calvin recognizes that his role as a song leader differs from Elise Witt's and Pete Seeger's, who, he charged, are exemplary models of leading groups in spontaneous singing. Calvin's method relies on teaching songs over time to a group of people. Calvin is especially fond of labor leader Joe Hill's statement: "A pamphlet, no matter how good, is never read more than once, but a song is learned by heart and repeated over and over." Through repetition and group singing, Calvin aims for songs to become part of people's lives, especially if those songs relate to a person's spiritual or political consciousness. Calvin often introduces songs within a historical framework so that participants more readily grasp the significance of their use in a particular setting. After all, Calvin urged, echoing Witt's sentiments, songs have work to do. Like Witt, Calvin also understands the value of having people sing together: "To have people breathe together and sing together means that people are moving together." For Calvin, "moving together" might mean people singing along, or "wiggling their butts," or joining together in common cause. If any or all of these are accomplished, the song has done its job.

A self-described untrained musician, Calvin eagerly admits that Pete Seeger influenced his musical journey, especially Seeger's 1963 concert recorded at Carnegie Hall, *We Shall Overcome*. For Calvin, Seeger's balance of powerful rhythm, expert group leadership, and rich lyrical content demonstrates the powerful appeal of movement music.

Perhaps Seeger was right: he believed that songs can help the world survive. However, he was realistic about how much songs can accomplish: "Songs won't save the planet. But, then, neither will books or speeches . . . Songs are sneaky things. They can slip across borders. Proliferate in prisons. Penetrate hard shells."[143] Seeger was fond of recalling Plato's ideas about the power of song: "Watch music. It's an important art form. Rulers should be careful about what songs are allowed to be sung."[144]

CHAPTER EIGHT
POWER AND UNITY THROUGH SACRIFICE AND STRUGGLE

When homeless people moved into the hotel, the protesters believed that power must be shared. Over time, a leadership team, named the Executive Committee, solidified among the homeless occupiers. Until the latter stages of the occupation, PUJ and the Executive Committee worked together in unity. They struggled collaboratively, their meetings were open, and power was shared.

Eduard commented, "There was this dynamic of wanting to do this within our own values and wanting to have grassroots leadership. We wanted to maintain what we believed in and what we were doing with our lives at the Open Door, but we also wanted to do this in partnership with homeless people." Homeless occupiers and activist occupiers labored to speak with a united voice.[145]

In retrospect, Carol Schlicksup believes that better communication among PUJ, the Executive Committee, and homeless people would have made the occupation a more satisfying experience. She believes the interaction was difficult because of the nature of the occupation as it took on a life of its own. It was important that the voices of homeless people were heard. "It was fitting," Carol exclaimed, "with the two groups inside, you wouldn't want the homeless people not to have a piece of being in charge. But it made coordinating things difficult . . . But there's always that tension because the homeless people lived it. They lived it. I didn't live it."

Rev. Nibs Stroupe leads prayer in the streets during the occupation. Photo by Gladys Rustay, courtesy of the Open Door Community.

Carol thinks that despite some problems, ideas and power were shared during the occupation. Further, "If anybody got left out of the communication, I preferred it be me and those like me. We weren't doing the occupation to glorify the Open Door. We were doing it to make a statement so there would be changes made for people who are homeless, so far better that they take more of the lead. I do think power was shared." Sister Jo Ann Geary believes that opening the door and welcoming homeless people was a good decision because of how people joined together and showed responsibility and leadership.

Despite some disagreements, "we really became a community," Eduard charged. "Didn't we become a community named Welcome House?" Elizabeth

Rev. Houston Wheeler, left, and Joe Beasley participate in a street action during the occupation. Photo courtesy of the Open Door Community.

Dede agreed and added, "I remember I wanted the name to be Welcome Home because I loved the play on words, so that is what I suggested, and the Executive Committee wanted it to be Welcome House." In an earlier letter to John Portman, PUJ remarked that they had changed the name of the hotel to Welcome Home. Elizabeth remembered that Maynard Jackson was in Chicago when people were deciding what to name the hotel. She recalled that when he first visited the hotel, people chanted, "Welcome Home, Maynard! Welcome Home!" By Wednesday of the first week, the Executive Committee and PUJ settled on Welcome House as the name.

The occupants remained in the hotel and used the press to inform and educate the general public, the business community, and political leaders about homelessness. But forces were exerted that required Mayor Jackson to take measures to remove the occupants.

Nelson Mandela and the Fourth of July Parade

One of those forces was Nelson Mandela's upcoming visit to Atlanta. The *Revolutionary Worker* newspaper summarized Mayor Jackson's predicament: "One big factor the city has been up against is the fact that this takeover was going on at the same time as the city was preparing for Nelson Mandela's June 27 visit. And city officials certainly didn't want to launch a massive police raid against over 200 homeless people just as Atlanta was greeting Mandela and posing as the 'City of Civil Rights.'"[146]

The Imperial occupation aside, Mandela's arrival in the city had already affected Atlanta's homeless-activist community. Mandela was scheduled

Rev. Hosea Williams talks to reporters during the Imperial Hotel occupation.
Photo courtesy of the Open Door Community.

to speak at Bobby Dodd Stadium on the campus of Georgia Institute of Technology. Civil rights activist and former city councilman Rev. Hosea Williams announced his plan for a march from the Imperial Hotel to the stadium to rally poor people who could not afford the $5.00 ticket, a sum too high for poor people.[147] A flyer circulated indicating that there would be a march from the "Home of the Homeless – Super-Rich Portman's Imperial Hotel" to Bobby Dodd Stadium. Williams and others wanted to bring attention to the idea that city leaders were claiming they wanted to help poor black people in South Africa, but the protesters asserted they were ignoring people at home. "The homeless have no place to sleep and the hungry have nothing to eat," the flyer charged.[148] By pushing Mandela to "demand that black leaders stop fighting among themselves and get together and help poor people here," the marchers believed they were "keeping Dr. King's true dream alive."

Tension increased when the Imperial Hotel occupants revealed that they would not join the march led by Williams.[149] The Executive Committee distributed a flyer of their own indicating their position on the issue. Their focus, the occupants explained, was housing for the homeless. But they made an effort to show that they supported Williams's protest, despite remaining inside the hotel instead of marching in solidarity. The announcement read in part:

> We have spoken with a representative of the Mandela reception committee and invited Mr. Mandela to visit us at Welcome House. We know that this invitation is being seriously considered and we are hopeful that it can be arranged. It is not, however, our intention to protest or in any way to take attention away from Mr. Mandela's important struggle on behalf of the people of South Africa. At this particular time it is not *our* mission to march but to say we are *here* in this building and shall *not* be moved . . . Let us stand together! Let us work together![150]

Mayor Jackson clearly did not want the protesters inside the Imperial when Nelson Mandela visited Atlanta. If the activists remained at the hotel, this would be a major embarrassment for Jackson's administration. Houston Wheeler contended that Nelson Mandela's impending visit to Atlanta altered the city's plans and hastened negotiations: "They thought, 'We've got

Homeless demonstrators in front of the Imperial Hotel. A handwritten sign reads "Homelessness is Not a Crime – An Empty Building Is! Defend Welcome House." Photo by Dwight Ross, Jr. Copyright *Atlanta Journal-Constitution.* Photo courtesy of Georgia State University.

to deal with his visit and this is more of a priority than the Imperial Hotel.'" Despite the city's desire to minimize the effects of the hotel occupation on their time and energy, Houston said, it had required more resources than they expected.

Another event, too, served as a catalyst to end the occupation: the July Fourth "Salute 2 America" parade. This parade, sponsored by WSB-TV Channel 2, was for many years the largest televised Independence Day parade in the United States. Its route traversed Peachtree Street in front of the Imperial Hotel. The city certainly did not want parade-goers and television viewers to witness the hotel occupants' continuing protest. Moreover, with the city expecting to blast out its "Atlanta Olympic Bid" campaign on July 4, they certainly did not want the hotel activists "raining on their parade."[151]

Carol Schlicksup said, "I had a clear sense that it would be great to stay for the parade, but that our time was probably pretty limited as it got closer." She believed that to have the occupation aired on television and have the activists interviewed as the parade went by would be devastating for the city and the Jackson administration. Though there was no clear ultimatum or specific date that occupants would be forced to leave, Carol and the others knew they would likely be forced out before the fourth.

Joe Beasley hoped that the evacuation of the hotel would be based on explorations of moral authority and political clout. He believed there needed to be a situation in which "Maynard Jackson, homeless advocates, and the homeless themselves could get together in one place and sit down and see if they could find a way where everybody's a winner." According to Joe, at this point, PUJ decided that it needed an exit strategy.

Jackson agreed to meet with the occupiers to discuss their demands. This meeting would be an opportunity for the protesters to articulate their demands and use their leverage before exiting the hotel, which they knew they would eventually do – by arrest or by successful negotiation.

CHAPTER NINE
NEGOTIATIONS AND COLLAPSE

R ev. Cameron Alexander served as a "third-party mediator" for the
meetings with Jackson, hosting the meetings at his west-Atlanta
congregation, Antioch Baptist Church North, about one mile from the hotel.
Some members of PUJ and the Executive Committee attended. Eduard
asserted that permanent, affordable housing instead of temporary shelter
was the only viable settlement that must be reached, and that 5,000 units
of SRO housing must be created, but he decided to remove himself from
head-to-head negotiations based on his belief that the Executive Committee
should bargain for homeless people. He was confident that the solidarity
forged inside the hotel among homeless people and housed activists would
prevail at the negotiating table.[152]

Houston Wheeler remembered that negotiations between the hotel
occupants and Jackson were a rallying point that brought people together
from various communities who were concerned about homelessness. The
majority of Atlanta's homeless people were black, and the African American
community played a crucial role in the negotiations.

When negotiations began, the Executive Committee made three
demands: 1) produce 3,500 units of SRO housing before Jackson's term
ended in three and a half years, with the first 200 units reserved for homeless
Imperial occupiers and, until those 200 were ready for occupancy, allow 75
of the homeless occupiers to live rent-free at the Atlanta Hotel for a month
and then have a 50 percent discount for the remaining time there; 2) create
a nine-person SRO oversight committee with broad authority over the
development and management of the projected units, with homeless people

and their advocates forming a significant portion of the committee; 3) loosen zoning ordinances so SROs could be built in areas where they were currently prohibited, and 4) require two new units of SRO housing to be built for every one that had been demolished.[153]

Charles Steffen pointed out that in the counterproposal drafted by Jackson's assistant and future two-term Atlanta mayor Shirley Franklin, the city maneuvered to shift the focus from permanent housing to temporary shelter. Further, even though it would strive to pass more favorable SRO ordinances while simultaneously pursuing state and county funding, the city would set a target of 1,000 to 2,000 new SRO units instead of 3,500. Additionally, the city's counterproposal was silent about the Executive Committee's goal for seats on the SRO oversight committee – a significant deletion, considering that homeless people feared that their voices would not be heard during development and management of SRO housing. Finally, the counterproposal did not commit to providing immediate housing for homeless occupiers.[154]

In a brilliant move, Franklin deflected the Executive Committee's scorn for her counterproposal when she lured Carl Hartrampf, a newly-hired member of the Atlanta Chamber of Commerce's Housing Resource Center, to attend the negotiations. Although eager to explore low-income housing credits and to experiment with rent-for-work programs, Hartrampf did not have any solid plans for affordable housing at the time of the meeting. When Franklin asked him to detail what the chamber was doing about affordable housing, his faltering attempts to explain his raw ideas were answered by the Executive Committee with declarations that he was scheming to create a new form of slavery. Steffen explained why Franklin's move was so savvy: "She understood the political dynamics in the room. The homeless men who had risen to prominence in the Executive Committee hoped to formalize their positions in the oversight committee, but Franklin and the city denied them this role, a psychological blow to their quest for power, legitimacy, and, not least important, manhood. They needed to project their disappointment on someone, and who better than the white representative of the Chamber of Commerce?"[155]

Ultimately, in an effort to get the Executive Committee to agree to leave the hotel, the city made some concessions. In response to the Executive Committee's first demand, the city agreed to the target goal of 3,500 units of SRO housing by the end of Jackson's term. This was an easy concession because it was framed in a way that indicated the city would make a good faith effort to reach this goal. The city did not, however, agree to house occupiers at the Atlanta Hotel. In response to the Executive Committee's demand for oversight on the SRO committee, with a significant number of seats held by homeless people and homelessness activists, the city enlarged the number of seats from nine to seventeen, and limited the committee to an advisory role instead of an oversight role. The Executive Committee's demand that the city liberalize SRO ordinances was favorably received, and the city agreed to urge the city council to address this issue. The city would only agree to a one-to-one replacement for demolished SRO housing.

After negotiators took a break just before 11:00 p.m. on July 2, People for Urban Justice returned to the negotiation table to learn that the Executive Committee had struck a deal with Franklin that they would leave the hotel and take jobs at the new shelter. Knowing that the Executive Committee would not be pleased with the city's partial concessions, Franklin sweetened the pot by offering them jobs. She had been secretly meeting with them, apparently planning this strategy. If the Executive Committee agreed to sign the proposal, Bill Jones would be named director of the newly-opening, though temporary, shelter on Memorial Drive. The remaining Executive Committee members would be put on the payroll in staff positions at five dollars an hour. Further, the Executive Committee would be given oversight of the shelter's daily operations. In a move to keep solidarity among homeless occupiers and homeless leaders – that is, in an effort to dispel the notion that the leadership group had been "bought off" – Jackson's administration

Outside the Imperial Hotel during the occupation. Photo by Dwight Ross, Jr. Copyright Atlanta Journal-Constitution. Photo courtesy of Georgia State University.

announced that one-half of the homeless occupiers had completed job applications in the city's water, sanitary, and highways and streets bureaus.[156] Only a handful of the applicants were employed through this tactic, but by offering gainful employment "the city . . . peel[ed] off the collective resolve of the occupiers."[157]

Soon after PUJ became aware of the agreement between Franklin and the Executive Committee, they learned that buses were scheduled to arrive the next day, Tuesday, July 3, to transport homeless hotel occupants to the new shelter. The permanent Welcome House structure at 234 Memorial Drive was still under construction, but a nearby temporary structure was ready for short-term habitation.

The Executive Committee and PUJ had spoken of their belief that the goal for permanent housing rather than temporary shelter was a cornerstone of the occupation. In an effort to represent Welcome House in a more positive light, the city engaged in various "rhetorical exercises" to disguise that it was a shelter.[158] The city proclaimed that Welcome House was a shelter but not a traditional one: "It will stay open 20 hours a day; it will provide lockers and security; it will provide some medical services; it will provide day labor services; it will have separate accommodations for men and women."[159] Leadership of and access to this non-traditional shelter, along with concessions to the Executive Committee's demands, were enough to pry the Executive Committee from the hotel. They signed the agreement. For the leaders of the homeless occupiers, who had certainly been for far too long denied voice and access to traditional forms of power, this deal was good enough: it was a positive response to their demands, and it appeared that it could garner both immediate and long-term improvements in their lives, and that was no small feat.

PUJ and the Executive Committee shared power inside the hotel, and though there was occasional friction, in general they collaborated with one goal in mind: affordable housing for all. But after over two weeks together, their collaboration had been unexpectedly broken apart. With the "Salute 2 America" parade looming and Nelson Mandela's visit imminent, Jackson and the occupants attempted to resolve the situation. But while PUJ negotiated openly with Jackson and his administration, the Executive Committee had been negotiating clandestinely with Franklin.

Eduard Loring did not mince words: "Shirley Franklin, who is a snake, came in and offered a financial temptation too difficult to refuse, and the

Executive Committee took a bite of it." Part of the agreement was that the Executive Committee would leave the hotel, which would likely hasten the departure of the remaining occupants.

It was a difficult moment when PUJ learned of the secret negotiations. Murphy Davis recalled that some members of the Executive Committee were embarrassed: "I don't think we will ever forget the moment that Bill Jones had to turn to us, look us in the eyes, and say 'I'm sorry, we're going with this offer for shelter, because we have accepted jobs there.'" PUJ members were deeply shocked. Eduard exclaimed, "We didn't know what the hell he was talking about."

Murphy recalled that she watched the occupation collapse in less than five minutes. The tough part was that negotiations had been going on for three days, and then without warning the landscape for PUJ negotiations had dramatically and irrevocably changed: "We realized in that awful moment that the legs had been completely cut out from under us as the political initiators, and the terrible meaning of that." She described the scene like it was "an overwhelming flash."

Murphy and the others learned something critical from this turn of events:

> It is difficult for people who are homeless to negotiate with powerful decision-makers. The process of negotiation assumes at least two parties – each with some sort of power base. When you have nothing and no power you are inclined to take anything because anything is better than nothing. The city represented the power of the state – economic power, the power to frame the issues, and the power of the police and criminal control system. The homeless poor brought only their own bodies and their overwhelming need – nothing more. Because the city (Shirley Franklin) could offer them something more than nothing, she was able to break the precious trust and solidarity that we had labored to build and nurture.

The clandestine negotiations between Franklin and the Executive Committee taught Murphy about power. Eduard added, "This was a 'growing-up' moment for us filled with sorrow and sadness and anguish."

Murphy said, "We really believed that we were going to get real housing for the folks in the Imperial. And we could have. I believe up to this day that we could have, had Shirley Franklin not bought off the leadership. And we did not know until right at the end of the negotiations that they had been bought off." After the occupation ended, Murphy wrote, "Franklin came in as an agent of lies and manipulation. She was dishonest from the first word and bought and sold homeless people without mercy. She manipulated the entire situation to the advantage of the mayor's office."[160]

PUJ was also shocked to discover that the jobs offered to the Executive Committee were at the new shelter, Welcome House. The name, drawn from the hotel occupation, was particularly stinging for PUJ. Almost worse was that the jobs offered to the Executive Committee paid only minimum wage.

A sense of betrayal cast a pall over PUJ. The deal brokered between Franklin and the Executive Committee undercut PUJ's central goal: to increase Atlanta's affordable housing stock. Eduard believed that because the occupation was unexpected, no one had a plan when they went to the negotiation table, and this hampered their ability to have all of their demands met. Eduard asserted that problems arose from holding the negotiations outside of Welcome House. By pulling the leadership out of the hotel for extended periods of time, unity and order were disrupted. Additionally, even though they had a very good housing negotiator through two and a half days of negotiations, a replacement was brought in on the third day who was less capable of handling negotiations.

After the occupation ended, Murphy contacted her friend Jack Boger, who was an NAACP Legal Defense Fund attorney in New York and said, "Jack, I want the names of the two or three best housing negotiators in this country, because we have just made the biggest mistake we have ever made." Reflecting on the abrupt end of negotiations, Murphy claimed that PUJ should have used negotiators who were much more capable of handling these matters – perhaps experts from outside of Atlanta. "We're not negotiators," she acknowledged.

Murphy described the post-negotiation scene as one in which the activists were isolated in a way that people would find difficult to understand: "You can't go out and explain that to the press because it is a very nuanced and complicated thing and that is where Shirley Franklin is so brilliant. She cut us off so we looked like the fools, like the uncooperative ones. The homeless people were cheering this great victory and we knew it wasn't a true victory."

Murphy said Franklin was able to disrupt solidarity because she was "smart as hell." Eduard added, "And progressives in this city love her. They don't know her. If you work with the poorest of the poor, you see a different world." In Houston Wheeler's words, you see the "Other" Atlanta.

Dick Rustay and others at the Open Door were kept apprised of the situation through telephone calls and dispatches when food or other needs were delivered to the hotel: "We weren't involved in the negotiations. Those would usually go on at night, and after we dropped stuff off at the hotel we'd come back and get word. We knew they were trying to negotiate, and I think that's where we felt Shirley Franklin was a very shrewd operator in terms of the promises she made, and it was divide and conquer." Dick's memory of Franklin's role in the negotiations was clear: "She seemed to be the one who was trying to figure out what to do." Dick suggested that when Franklin stayed all night in the hotel talking to occupants, she hatched the plan to get them out. And it worked, although, Dick explained, "it turned out that most of the jobs ended or dead-ended, or most of the people didn't stay there."

Eduard's summary of Franklin's method was blunt: "She came up with a war plan and dropped a bomb." His anger and frustration was apparent as he pondered Franklin's eventual service as a two-term Atlanta mayor:

> We can't house the homeless because black politicians are owned by the white money makers. This is the reason we can't act for the homeless. Shirley Franklin, though black and Presbyterian, is no Harriet Tubman. She feels no commitment to the poor. Franklin, whom Andy Young named, "my secret weapon," is shrewd, but worse, she traded her black heritage for government porridge. She stabbed her homeless brothers and sisters in the back. She two-timed and double crossed them. Her agenda as mayor was to remove the poor, especially the black poor, from the city so white middle class and rich people could move in.

Houston Wheeler was sure that Portman did not want to be drawn into the fray of the occupation. City officials became the negotiators, he said, particularly Franklin: "She was one of Mayor Jackson's 'lieutenants' and their message consistently was, 'Alright, if you leave the building then we'll sit down and talk about affordable housing; the building is unsafe and you're at risk, and that's our concern.'" Houston recalled PUJ's strategy in response to the city's claim: "Sure, the building wasn't safe and it was filthy, but we used that as a way of prolonging it to the degree that the city would come around and make some concessions." Had Franklin not brokered the deal with the Executive Committee, and had the occupants remained in the hotel, perhaps the concessions would have been greater.

Atlanta Municipal Court Judge Andrew Mickle was not surprised that Franklin was involved in the negotiating process. According to Mickle, Franklin knew the office well because she was the de facto mayor during Andrew Young's terms as mayor (1982-1990) while he was traveling the world promoting Atlanta: "[She] was doing a lot of the hands-on, daily stuff that the mayor would otherwise do."[161] In sum, Franklin was politically astute by the time she was involved in the Imperial Hotel occupation. "She's very smart and calculating," Mickle observed. She "knew what she wanted to achieve and she could be very forceful. She knew how to get things done. Some would call her ruthless."

As a "consummate political insider" after having served as commissioner of cultural affairs during Jackon's first two mayoral terms and then as chief administrative officer and city manager during Young's two terms, Franklin, Charles Steffen asserts, "had the best grasp of the political forces at play" during the occupation. During her years at city hall, Franklin "learned to move with equal comfort among black officials, white CEOs, political activists, and poor people," so it is no misnomer when Mayor Young called her "my secret weapon."[162] Steffen observes that it is impossible to know exactly what was discussed when Franklin repeatedly entered the hotel to talk with the Executive Committee and homeless occupiers. Based on subsequent events, it appears that Franklin exited the hotel the final time "armed with a bargaining strategy . . . to isolate the Executive Committee from PUJ, leveraging the divisions between the white religious activists and the homeless black occupiers to achieve a settlement favorable to the interests of city hall and the business community."[163] In the days that followed, she oversaw all aspects of negotiations.[164]

The way the occupation ended caused a significant rift between homeless people and PUJ activists when, following the agreement between Franklin and the Executive Committee, the homeless occupants consented to leave the hotel. This agreement hastened the eventual arrest of six of the initial eight PUJ activists who entered the building two weeks earlier.

When the Executive Committee agreed to the pact with Franklin, PUJ lost its leverage; PUJ's power was bound up in occupying the hotel. They had achieved leverage through bodily protest, and had communicated their grievances through the media. Francis Fox Piven explains the relationship between power and disruptive actions:

> Protest movements do try to communicate their grievances, of course, with slogans, banners, antics, rallies, marches, and so on. They do this partly to build the movement and its morale, and partly to appeal for allies. The reverberations of disruptive actions, the shutdowns or highway blockages or property destruction, are inevitably also communicative. But while disruption thus usually gives the protesters voice, voice alone does not give the protesters much power."[165]

PUJ had achieved voice, and it had achieved power, but they lost both when the Executive Committee agreed to leave the hotel.

The occupation had to end; it could not continue forever. Modern governments, "locked into complex societal systems of cooperation and interdependency," must respond to disruptions because "state authority and power ultimately depend on the relatively smooth functioning of societal patterns of cooperation."[166] Moreover, ruling groups are generally "better positioned to take advantage of new conditions and to adapt their strategies of contestation . . . They ordinarily have the advantage in contests that require endurance."[167]

It appears that Franklin's backroom deals and savvy deflections illuminated a truth that she knew all too well and that PUJ learned in defeat: people who have nothing will take anything.[168] The rumored July 2nd deadline, Jackson's political astuteness, and Franklin's deft maneuvering created a situation where the threat of arrest and the allure of jobs "carried the day." [169] The homeless occupiers' brazen defiance of the city's political and business establishment screeched to a halt when they lost one of their few formidable weapons: the power to disrupt.[170]

CHAPTER TEN
COMPROMISING AND
DEFIANT DEPARTURES

City officials were pleased after it was announced that the Executive Committee had accepted the offer to leave the Imperial to take jobs operating Welcome House. Mayor Jackson and Executive Committee member Bill Jones announced the agreement to jubilant cheers among homeless people and city administrators. Jackson told reporters that over the next three and one-half years, 3,500 units of affordable housing would be built. He did not, however, indicate how much the housing would cost or where it would be built. "The point is we've got a problem here and Atlanta is in the forefront of trying to solve it," he reasoned.[171] A newspaper report indicated that the city averted what it thought would be a "nasty confrontation" by beating a July 2 midnight deadline to end the occupation, a deadline that PUJ activists did not know existed.[172]

During the sixteen-day hotel occupation, Mayor Jackson's attention was directed to issues related to homelessness and affordable housing. After the agreement between the city and the Executive Committee was announced, Angelo Fuster, the mayor's spokesperson, extolled the positive outcome of the negotiations. He proclaimed, "The mayor believes that we have negotiated in good faith and have achieved quite a lot for the homeless."[173] Shirley Franklin commented that with over 10,000 homeless people in Atlanta, "It's been a crisis for a long time, but their demonstration has made us sit up and take notice."[174] Bill Jones declared that the takeover had done more in two weeks for homeless people than committees had done in seven years.[175]

A scene on the final day of the Imperial Hotel occupation, July 3, 1990. Photo by Dwight Ross, Jr. Copyright *Atlanta Journal-Constitution*. Photo courtesy of Georgia State University.

Several positive things did, indeed, happen during the occupation and negotiations. For example, the city delayed a vote on a proposed SRO ordinance that would have blocked construction of many (if not all) SROs. Mayor Jackson vowed that he would aggressively oppose the ordinance. Jackson also said he would relax zoning restrictions and create legislation to discourage developers from demolishing buildings that could be renovated for SROs.[176] Jackson's plan would require that for every room destroyed, another would be created. Additionally, in what appeared to be an effort to meet more of PUJ's and the Executive Committee's demands, Mayor Jackson's administration speedily introduced measures to the city council that would provide $638,000 to build or refurbish nearly 300 units of SRO housing.[177] It was also announced that Welcome House would be open 20 hours a day and that it would have more relaxed rules than other shelters, especially those associated with entering and leaving the facility.[178]

A street preacher ourside of the Imperial Hotel on the final day of the occupation. Photo by Dwight Ross, Jr. Copyright *Atlanta Journal-Constitution*. Photo courtesy of Georgia State University.

Eduard Loring ready to speak into a megaphone from the ledge of the Imperial Hotel on the final day of the occupation. Photo by Dwight Ross, Jr. Copyright *Atlanta Journal-Constitution*. Photo courtesy of Georgia State University.

PUJ was now aware that the police would arrest and charge with criminal trespass anyone who remained in the hotel after the buses departed for Welcome House. Despite being shocked and disappointed by what had transpired between Franklin and the Executive Committee, six of the initial eight PUJ members who entered the building on June 18 chose to remain in the hotel and get arrested. Their arrest would cement their commitment to the action and bring additional media attention to it.

C.M. Sherman and Larry Travick chose not to get arrested. Murphy Davis suggested that this decision divided opinion among the activists: "Elizabeth felt betrayed, but I felt it was very important not to use that language with C.M. and Larry because both of them had been homeless. They were at the bottom of everything for years before the occupation, and I felt it was very unfair of us as white people who had always been privileged to expect them to take that on."

Murphy emphasized the complexity of the issue and the different ways she and Elizabeth viewed C.M. and Larry's decision not to get arrested:

> Homeless people left with cheers of victory. The night before, they had held a press conference and they were claiming an enormous victory. We knew that it was *not* an enormous victory. We thought that it was absolute betrayal by the city, so I felt like it was very important for C.M. and Larry to have the space to say "no, we're not going to go forward at this point. "We were very glad that John Flournoy went with us, but Elizabeth and I were at a very different place at that point. And we argued about it some. I didn't want C.M. and Larry disrespected for not going with us.

Elizabeth insisted she was not disrespectful toward C.M. and Larry, two men with whom she collaborated in a dramatic struggle for affordable housing.

Even though some PUJ members felt a sense of betrayal, Carol Schlicksup did not. When she learned of the deal that homeless people made with city officials, she was prepared to leave the hotel. "I totally understood," she said. She also believed that the departure of homeless people did not undercut PUJ's goals. Carol knew the agreement had been signed for the development of SRO housing, and she hoped housing would be built, but she also realized it was only a promise: "I didn't believe for one minute that the agreement meant all was smooth, but I felt like it was something. I certainly understood homeless people leaving – absolutely. I just wasn't certain that what we had hoped for was going to happen at all, and I figured it wasn't going to happen anytime soon."

Left: Five members of the initial "Imperial Eight" watch from a ledge as events unfold on the final day of the occupation. Photo by Dwight Ross, Jr. Copyright *Atlanta Journal-Constitution*. Photo courtesy of Georgia State University.

Below: Dick Rustay at street level holding a sign in front of the Imperial Hotel on the final day of the occupation. Photo by Dwight Ross, Jr. Copyright *Atlanta Journal-Constitution*. Photo courtesy of Georgia State University.

The evacuation of the hotel began early Tuesday morning, July 3. Around 7:00 a.m. homeless people inside the hotel began gathering their belongings in preparation for their bus ride to Welcome House.[179] By noon, roughly 85 homeless people had taken the bus to the new, temporary shelter.[180] Stanley Gibson, a homeless person who joined the protesters inside the hotel during the occupation, remembered taking a bus to Welcome House: "It was like a school bus. I was on that first bus that went down. I was interviewed by the news and before we got there another news station was there. They filmed us getting off the bus and going into the warehouse."

Stanley confirmed that the temporary Welcome House was not ready for occupation. Inside the structure there was open space with makeshift dividers. Men were situated on one side of the dividers; women and children were on the other side. He said that the bathroom was "kind of open" until they made more progress during the evolving construction process. John Scruggs, another homeless person who joined the protesters inside the hotel during the occupation and was later transported to Welcome House by bus, reported, "It was like a tent-shed. There were army cots in there and a lot of people and it started overflowing."

Bill Jones expressed strong emotions about leaving the Imperial Hotel. He declared, "It became a part of us. We developed a community. It's really like leaving home. It's like heading out into the unknown."[181] At the new shelter, Jones spoke optimistically about partitioning the large rooms to enhance privacy. That was unlikely to happen soon: city officials

A school bus awaits Imperial Hotel occupants who decided to go to Welcome House, the homeless shelter on Memorial Drive. Photo by Dwight Ross, Jr. Copyright *Atlanta Journal-Constitution*. Photo courtesy of Georgia State University.

Left: People boarding a bus that will take them from the Imperial Hotel to Welcome House shelter. Photo by Dwight Ross, Jr. Copyright *Atlanta Journal-Constitution*. Photo courtesy of Georgia State University.

Right: People aboard the first bus headed to Welcome House shelter. Photo by Dwight Ross, Jr. Copyright *Atlanta Journal-Constitution*. Photo courtesy of Georgia State University.

announced that they had already spent $75,000 on the shelter and there was no money left for additional improvements.[182]

Later, after the occupation and after initial feelings of shock, disappointment, and bitterness faded, some PUJ members believed that it was best to support the decision of homeless people to move into the new shelter. Homeless peoples' decisions, they thought, were often made from multiple bad choices. For housed members of PUJ, the shelter was not what they had demanded during the occupation, but they knew that they themselves would go home to housing, and that they had no right to judge others for choosing housing – even if it was a temporary shelter. An anonymous PUJ member wrote, "The time of distinction has come to support the decision of the homeless folks to choose the better of several bad options. No matter what is done to the Memorial Drive Shelter, it's still a shelter. A shelter is not real housing." After the occupation ended, Eduard urged PUJ members to visit the new Welcome House to give moral support to the homeless people staying there.[183]

Arrests

Eduard Loring, Murphy Davis, Elizabeth Dede, John Flournoy, Carol Schlicksup, and Jo Ann Geary refused to leave the hotel silently. Despite being disappointed by the Executive Committee's decision to leave, they remained inside and maintained the integrity of their original purpose – to fight for affordable housing for all.[184]

The protesters knew that after the Executive Committee and the homeless people left, everybody else would be arrested. Jo Ann thought

Left: Marcella Maguire, with People for Urban Justice, comforting Anderson McCormick, who departed from the Imperial Hotel on the final day of the occupation. Photo by Dwight Ross, Jr. Copyright *Atlanta Journal-Constitution*. Photo courtesy of Georgia State University.

Right: Police officers Captain W.F. Derrick, Officer J.E. Harrison, and Lieutenant H.L Johnson, standing near the front entrance of the Imperial Hotel on the final day of the occupation. Photo by Dwight Ross, Jr. Copyright *Atlanta Journal-Constitution*. Photo courtesy of Georgia State University.

that they were told they would be arrested if they did not clear out of the hotel after the buses departed with the occupants.[185] She added, "I was not leaving. We came too far." Additionally, she found comfort in her friend Gay Dellinger's remark that she would put up her property, including a 10-acre vineyard in Cartersville, Georgia, as bail for all eight PUJ occupants, if they needed it.

After watching the departure of the homeless protesters with whom they had shared the hotel for sixteen days, the remaining group padlocked two chains on the front gate. Eduard recalled: "We all spent time on the roof of the front porch. We were very close to the street. We had the bullhorn and we were yelling and crying out all morning."

People for Urban Justice once again demanded a meeting with John Portman and delivered a letter that morning that said:

> Two weeks ago People for Urban Justice hand-delivered a letter to you, asking for communication and a meeting with you. We also told you at that time that we were occupying the Imperial Hotel and would continue to do so until affordable housing for the homeless and the poor was provided by the business community. During the two weeks that we have occupied the Imperial Hotel, it has been a Welcome House for as many as 350 homeless people.

Today, they will leave the building to live in a shelter because they were threatened with arrest on the charge of criminal trespass. These members of the Welcome House family will not move into the affordable housing we have demanded. Where are you, Mr. Portman? People for Urban Justice continue to wait for a meeting with you. Please join us in the Imperial Hotel and send your construction crews to renovate it as permanent affordable housing for the homeless. House the homeless here![186]

Portman never arrived, but his representatives did, along with police officers. At 12:40 p.m. on Tuesday, July 3, firefighters used a chain cutter to remove the chains on the front gate. The protesters were on the rooftop over the front entrance, and the police met them there. After a brief discussion, the protesters were escorted to the entry of the hotel. Neal Kamin, an attorney for Portman, explained what happened: "We asked them to leave. When they refused, we asked the police to arrest them."[187] He added, "We were given a notice from the city that the building is unsafe . . . We were merely complying with that order."[188] The protesters were charged with criminal trespass.

Carol summed up the final moments inside the hotel: "On the morning of July 3, sixteen days after the occupation of the Imperial Hotel began, and one day before the big Fourth of July parade would have passed by the occupied hotel, city police, with Mr. Portman's lawyer present, charged us with criminal trespass and arrested us."[189]

Eduard vividly remembered what happened when they were escorted out of the hotel: "The

Marcella Maguire of People for Urban Justice salvaging posters at the end of the Imperial Hotel occupation. Photo by Dwight Ross, Jr. Copyright *Atlanta Journal-Constitution.* Photo courtesy of Georgia State University.

police backed the van up and they arrested us. There was a picture of Elizabeth getting arrested, but they had worked it so we would not get very much publicity." Additionally, the press and bystanders were not present to see or speak to PUJ and Open Door supporters on the street. Murphy pointed out the city's strategy on their arrest and removal: "They waited until after prime-time news at noon and arrested us about one o'clock, after all the TV cameras were shut down." She explained, "They backed the police van right up to the door as close as they could get it so there would be no TV or other footage or photographs of us being escorted out of the door and into the police van."

Despite the city's strategy to prevent publicity of their arrest, Murphy explained that all of them tried to bring attention to the arrest and removal. For example, as they entered the police van accompanied by police but not handcuffed, the protesters shouted to nearby homeless people and passers-by. Murphy shouted, "House the homeless!" while flashing a peace sign. Eduard yelled sarcastically, "Mr. Portman's on the way!"[190]

After they were in the police van the activists assumed they were going to jail. Instead, they were taken to the parking lot of the Civic Center and booked. Then a van took them to the Open Door and released them in the driveway. Eduard declared, "It was quite another shock."

Jo Ann Geary remembered other details:

> We were arrested and they were asking about zip codes and Elizabeth, Murphy, Ed, and Carol lived at the Open Door. I did not. My zip code was different. I just had the thought, "Oh my goodness, they're all going to go into one paddy wagon and I'm going to go in another." And I didn't even know if I'd be going to the same place. And I remember for the first time being nervous, actually scared. It's awful to say but you don't know what the police or whoever will do if you are alone. But we all got into the same paddy wagon. They took us to the back of the Open Door. We did not go to jail.

The protesters were given a ticket and a court date. They were disappointed not to be jailed. Eduard explained, "We would have been welcomed to another 'home for the homeless' – jail. But they weren't about to let us get in that jail. We would have disrupted the hell out of it, because everybody watches television and everybody knew what was going on."

Day in Court

On July 18, 1990, one month after the initial eight People for Urban Justice activists broke into the hotel to bring attention to homelessness in Atlanta, six of them (Murphy, Eduard, John, Elizabeth, Carol, and Jo Ann) arrived in court and appeared in front of Judge Andrew Mickle. Carol reported that PUJ's attorneys, Brian Spears, Michael Hauptman, and Bruce Harvey, spoke eloquently in front of the judge. The protesters were charged with criminal trespass, and agreed to plead guilty to a lesser charge of disorderly conduct. Judge Mickle announced that he would suspend their $75 fines if the protesters used the money to "further [their] cause" and to never again be involved in a similar action on the Imperial property. The protesters agreed and, as "knowing smiles were exchanged," they jubilantly left the courtroom.[191] Jo Ann Geary believed they were fortunate in getting Judge Mickle to hear their case. She said, "I felt like this guy really does get it. He knows what we were about."

After Eduard stepped outside of the courtroom, he told reporters that he was expecting Mayor Jackson to keep his promise to break ground on an SRO property by September 1: "Any human being is [as] good as their word. Their word was they will break ground by Sept. 1. Our word is, if they don't, we'll be back in the streets." The central issue was not criminal trespassing, he exclaimed, but rather how the homeless would be housed. Shaking hands with well-wishers outside the courthouse, he continued, "The issue is how [we may] build the Beloved Community in this city where there is too much glitter and glass, and too much hunger and homelessness."[192]

In a playful gesture before the judge arrives on their day in court for their role in the Imperial Hotel occupation, Murphy Davis pretends to strangle Eduard Loring. Photo appeared in the October 7, 1999 *Atlanta Journal-Constitution.* Copyright *Atlanta Journal-Constitution.* Photo courtesy of Georgia State University.

When considering the occupation and the activists' subsequent day in court, Judge Mickle suggested that there are two ways to view how it was resolved: "Either both sides looked good, or neither side looked bad." If he is correct, then none of the players — PUJ, Jackson, or Portman — drew negative publicity. Mickle also believed that the police devised a deliberate strategy when they retrieved PUJ members from the hotel after the noon news broadcast. Also, when they backed up the van directly to the door and then delivered them to the Open Door, they "played it perfectly" because they denied them visibility and a platform to speak: "They weren't allowed to make the statement they were trying to make because of the way the arrest took place. The police didn't want to give them a pedestal from which to grandstand." Of course, Mickle added, "these were not violent people . . . they were not hurting anybody," so it made political sense to release them without putting them in jail.

Mickle also discussed the charge against PUJ members, which, he said, was appropriate: "We don't have breaking and entering in Georgia; there's no such thing. It's either burglary or trespassing. A definition of burglary is entering a dwelling or a business of another without authority with the intent to steal or commit a felony while you're in there." Burglary is a one- to twenty-year felony charge. Mickle explained that "there was nothing in the hotel to steal because the place was a dump," so burglary would not have been the correct charge. In Georgia, criminal trespass is a misdemeanor with a one-to twelve-month jail sentence. However, Mickle urged, it is rare for someone to serve jail time for crimes against property; most get probation. Mickle also suggested that PUJ's actions were on a far less harmful level than what his court was seeing in 1990: rape, murder, armed robbery, child molestation, aggravated child molestation, and gang shootings.

In terms of danger to others, PUJ's violations were relatively minor, so it made sense that their charges were plea bargained from criminal trespass, a misdemeanor, to disorderly conduct, a city ordinance violation punishable by a maximum of 180 days and a $1,000 fine. Overall, Judge Mickle considered the plea bargain a "win-win" situation because the protesters made their statement in the hotel, the police did not forcibly drag anybody out, Portman did not look bad, and the city promised to build housing. He added that there has been a lot done to accommodate the homeless since then and "maybe that's where it got its jumpstart."

Judge Mickle recalled that this case was a simple one because there were no factual issues to decipher – it was all "up front"; that is, the facts were clear and PUJ members did not deny they had trespassed on private property. He also had no problem suspending their fines because, as he had done in other trespassing cases, he suspended fines for time served if the people had somewhere else to go. The hotel was in particularly bad shape, with no running water and other amenities, so he considered the protesters' sixteen-day occupation equivalent to jail time. Judge Mickle agreed to suspend the protesters' fines if they promised to never again be involved in a similar action on the Imperial property.[193] As he viewed it, there is an inalienable right to protest in the United States and knew that they would protest again, so he was careful about how he phrased his message. He recalled, "I couldn't say they couldn't protest. I knew damn well that they were going to be involved in something, so I had to qualify it." Jo Ann Geary recalled there was a "dramatic pause" when he told them not to protest at the Imperial again. Her interpretation suggested that Judge Mickle supported their efforts. "That couldn't be further from the truth," Mickle exclaimed. "I was trying to send the message that the cops aren't going to be so nice the next time. It's not going to be peaches and cream like it was this time."

And so it appears that Judge Mickle was aware of their cause and supported their right to protest, but was in no way sympathetic. In his words, just because he suspended their fines and agreed to a plea bargain, "That doesn't mean I necessarily agreed with them."

CHAPTER ELEVEN

TOO SLOW WITH THE SROs

Even though the Imperial Hotel occupation did not end as many PUJ members would have liked, they were energized about the possibility that affordable housing would be built. They believed they had made progress – that they had put a chink in the wall of domination.[194] But as months passed with little movement on SRO development, PUJ's hope turned to skepticism, and they responded with their words and their bodies.

PUJ returned to the Imperial Hotel nine months after the occupation. On March 19, 1991, they held a 10:00 a.m. press conference in front of the hotel, followed by a march to city hall and a rally. At the culmination of the rally, they presented the Memorandum of Understanding to Mayor Jackson – the document he had signed nine months previously. Speakers at the Imperial Hotel press conference included C.M. Sherman, Rev. Nibs Stroupe, Joe Beasley, Houston Wheeler, and Moriba Karamoko.[195]

One week prior to the city hall rally, PUJ honorary co-chair Francis Pauley invited Tom Teepen of the *Atlanta Constitution* to attend the press conference. In her letter to Teepen, Pauley pointed out that even though Mayor Jackson appeared sincere in his commitment to fulfilling the Memorandum of Understanding, substantive results had not transpired since occupants departed the hotel in July of 1990.[196] In a flyer announcing the press conference and rally, PUJ compared the lack of SRO progress to human gestation:

> We've waited nine long months! It's been a miscarriage of justice!
> On June 18, 1990, the homeless people of Atlanta and People

for Urban Justice took over the Imperial Hotel – an abandoned SRO facility. On July 3, 1990, Mayor Maynard Jackson signed a Memorandum of Understanding with those of us who occupied the building, promising 3,500 units of SRO housing. Today is March 19, 1991. We've waited nine months for the birth of justice in this city. No construction of new, affordable SRO housing has begun. It's been a miscarriage of justice! Please join us at city hall now as we bring this message to Mayor Maynard Jackson. House the Homeless![197]

PUJ's "Statement of Purpose" for the press conference underscored what little had been accomplished in the post-occupation period:

> The homeless people of this city, and People for Urban Justice as their advocates, have gotten little support or cooperation from the city of Atlanta and its business community. There are no new affordable SRO units, but we have heard a lot of rhetoric and excuses . . . We have come to tell the mayor, the people of Atlanta, and the world that we are damned tired of waiting and suffering![198]

African American community leader and partner of the Open Door Community, Phillip Williams, wrote: "Mr. Mayor Maynard Jackson, on behalf of People for Urban Justice, the homeless people of Atlanta, the three folks who burned to death at the Metroplex Club, and others who have died because they had no housing, we present to you a copy of the Memorandum of Understanding which you signed. So far you have failed in your commitment. Therefore, we are presenting this to you so that you can wake up and live up to your commitment."[199] Carol Schlicksup wrote:

> Mayor Jackson, we count on the fulfillment of your promises! We wait on your word! It's been nine long months since you signed this Memorandum of Understanding, nine months of waiting for your promise to be birthed! We are in pain! God's people, your people, citizens of Atlanta continue to die on the streets, continue to call the cramped, crowded, dehumanizing shelters home, continue to be housed in the city prisons and in Grady Hospital. Without a decent place to live, even just a single room to occupy,

it's impossible to keep a job, to learn and study, to stay physically and mentally healthy. Housing precedes employment, sobriety, education, and good health. What can we do for homeless people? Why don't we give them a home?! That's what you promised, Mayor Jackson, and the fruit of your promise is overdue! How long must we wait?!"[200]

In the press release, PUJ reiterated why they had occupied the hotel in June: to demand decent and affordable housing for Atlanta's homeless residents. They reminded Atlanta residents that Mayor Jackson had committed his administration to producing 1,000 SRO units per year, for three and a half years, with construction of the first units expected to begin no later than September 1, 1990. Those promises had not been kept, and while homeless people filled Atlanta's streets, shelters, and cat holes, the plans for providing housing for Olympic athletes and sporting events proceeded on schedule.

Moreover, PUJ argued, while the city had found funds for a temporary shelter, they had not yet secured funding for transitional and affordable housing. Particularly galling was the fact that the city spent $75,000 to open Welcome House, as well as funding a shelter in the city hall annex and one in the former jail on Jefferson Street, while the Bethlehem Inn, a 60-unit SRO near the Atlanta-Fulton County Stadium that had been under construction for five years, was still unfinished. By 1991, the Bethlehem Inn had cost the city $800,000.[201]

This event was designed to compel Mayor Jackson to move forward at a less glacial pace on SRO development. But some residents believed that PUJ was too critical of Mayor Jackson. Responding to an April 2, 1991, *Atlanta Constitution* letter written by Sherry Sanders, director of the Atlanta Office of Human Services, about PUJ's negative critique of the Jackson administration, PUJ activist Phillip Williams responded:

People for Urban Justice operates with different strategies and with a faster timetable than Ms. Sanders and the mayor's office are accustomed to. We are a political action group, and while we attend meetings, we also take over buildings and march on city hall. We want to believe Mayor Jackson's fine promises to the homeless people of this city. Last July he promised 3,500 SRO units in three and a half years, with groundbreaking to begin on September 1, 1990. It is now April 1991. No groundbreaking has occurred, and People for Urban Justice finds itself saying, with all due respect to Mayor Jackson and Sherry Sanders, "You are too slow with the SROs!"[202]

Good News and Bad News, 1990–1991

PUJ monitored progress – or more aptly, lack of progress – in the months and years following the occupation. Houston Wheeler, for example, compiled lists indicating significant events that transpired from September 1, 1990 (the unmet proposed deadline for groundbreaking of the first SRO project), to June 18, 1991 (the one-year anniversary of the initial day of the hotel occupation).[203] During this period there was *some* forward movement, but stasis largely prevailed.

On a positive note, by the end of September 1990, the city council had approved a location for the first SRO site (Welcome House) at Washington Street and Memorial Drive, and tax credits had been awarded to Progressive Redevelopment, Inc. (PRI) to develop the SRO. There was also progress in the SRO advisory committee. From October through December 1990 the committee met four times, and they worked with the Memorandum of Understanding, the signed document that ended the hotel occupation.[204]

On a more troubling note, the committee learned about snags in SRO land, finance, and construction processes that would undoubtedly slow development. In late 1990 PUJ met with Central Atlanta Progress president Joe Martin to solicit his support for the Welcome House SRO and to discuss permanent financing of SROs and affordable housing in general. PUJ encouraged CAP to use the Atlanta Equity Fund (AEF) to develop affordable housing. AEF was private-sector funding for the development of low and moderate income housing. In January of 1991, Mayor Jackson urged the city's business leaders to fully fund the AEF.[205]

In a controversial move, Jackson and the city council amended the zoning ordinance to require a special use permit for SROs. In this action and a few others, there was no consultation with the SRO advisory committee, and this contradicted the terms of the Memorandum of Understanding. Moreover, after receiving a draft of the city's proposed SRO production program, several members of PUJ and the advisory committee objected to it. They believed that it would segregate specific homeless populations according to mental and physical attributes and subsequently fail to address the dire need of SRO housing for single men, as indicated in the Memorandum of Understanding.[206]

In February of 1991, PRI reported that permanent financing had not yet been found for construction of the Welcome House SRO. In early April, the SRO advisory committee met with Mayor Jackson, who reaffirmed his commitment to produce 3,500 SRO units. By mid-April only six local corporations had made commitments to the Atlanta Equity Fund. By late April, at the twelfth meeting of the SRO advisory committee, permanent financing was still not in place for the Welcome House SRO.[207]

Yet another problem arose when the Atlanta City Council Development Committee criticized the city's proposed site for the Welcome House SRO because there was a liquor store adjacent to it.[208] The political geography of Welcome House was already controversial. Affordable housing developer Craig Taylor recalled that the original location was supposed to be several blocks away in a parking lot adjacent to Trinity United Methodist Church. Taylor believed this was a good location, yet despite the church having strong advocacy programs for homeless people, it was pulled from consideration. Taylor was disappointed to learn that a member of the congregation was a prominent city leader, and that what seemed to be back-room pressure dictated that another location be found.

June 18, 1991, marked the one-year anniversary of the occupation. Houston Wheeler noted that affordable housing development in Atlanta was moving at a snail's pace and that just one conclusion could be drawn from this: "The city and business community have other priorities which dominate the Atlanta scene. Olympic venues, the Georgia Dome stadium, and office towers like One Peachtree Center are constructed with city and corporate support, while housing for the poor is non-existent and stalled for lack of leadership."[209]

Another Return to the Imperial Hotel

Houston was especially active during post-occupation street actions, meetings, and disruptions, reacting to a climate that had returned to business-as-usual. Fifteen months after the occupation, on September 12,

1991, he took part in a follow-up action. As part of a larger campaign to get Mayor Jackson's attention (a campaign including buttons and banners, some that said "Break Ground or Break In: Back to the Imperial?"), Wheeler, Bruce Gunter of Progessive Redevelopment, and two others took a bold step: they broke into the Imperial Hotel.

The hotel doors were sealed with concrete block up to the second floor. Early in the morning while it was still dark, three from the group climbed to the third floor and entered a window. They remembered how small PUJ's banner appeared from the street in the 1990 occupation, so they made their banner much larger by sewing together six bed sheets.[210] The bright red lettering said, "Dear Maynard, Back to the Imperial? Keep Your Promise."[211] Unlike the original protesters (the "Imperial Eight") of June 1990, these advocates did not linger in the hotel – they broke in, hung the banner, and left. They had breakfast at an Atlanta landmark, the Majestic Diner, and then they called the media.[212]

A writer for the *Atlanta Journal-Constitution* reported that the banner served as a reminder of the past, and also a warning for the future.[213] The press was covering the mayor's speaking engagement at a nearby hotel that

A 1991 action at the Imperial Hotel. Photo courtesy of Progressive Redevelopment.

day, so they believed they could get the mayor's attention and perhaps even some press coverage. A newspaper story reported that Mayor Jackson was aware of the banner. The action had worked. Houston reflected, "It was less volatile than the original occupation, but it was still a good action." The names of the perpetrators remained unknown for many years after the incident.

One problem that tempered PUJ's hopes for SRO development was that the proposed 209-bed Welcome House SRO, with rooms that would rent for seven dollars a night, the "benchmark of affordability" for low wage workers, was mired in financial problems. Only 68 percent of the funding had been secured. Bruce Gunter believed the mayor could do more to find funding and expedite progress on the development. He said, "It just hasn't had the mayor's attention. Other things have crowded his agenda. I think people just wanted to send him a reminder."[214]

By late 1991, the Stratford Inn on Parkway near North Avenue was the only SRO to open since the occupation. Affordable housing advocates were frustrated, especially so because rent was about one hundred dollars a week at the Stratford, and this was higher than what the Executive Committee had negotiated in the Memorandum of Understanding that ended the occupation. Anita Beaty, executive director of Metro Atlanta Task Force for the Homeless, and executive board member of the National Coalition for the Homeless, argued that with twice as many people living in shelters in the summer of 1991 compared to 1990, people were frustrated with so little progress on SRO development. Mayor Jackson's spokesperson, Angelo Fuster, reported that the mayor shared people's frustration.[215] While it is true that the mayor's administration had been moving forward on SRO development, the pace was exceedingly slow.

Arrested at a Meeting

In another effort to bring attention to the glacial progress on SRO development, PUJ decided to disrupt a meeting at Central Atlanta Progress (CAP) in October 1991. CAP's mandate was the promotion, development, and expansion of the downtown central business district, the commercial heart of downtown. At the time of the protest, 180 local corporations were CAP members. At a CAP executive meeting to discuss SRO financing and development, over 30 activists carried signs in the streets reminding the mayor to keep his promise to develop affordable housing. Activists Denson Philips, Phillip Williams, Robert Abrams, and Houston Wheeler interrupted the meeting, and were arrested and charged with criminal trespass. They were held in the city jail in lieu of $551 bond.[216]

Disrupting the meeting was an effort to get CAP to sign a resolution pledging $4 million from the business community to help build affordable housing through the Atlanta Equity Fund. The protesters claimed that they did not believe the business community was serious about solving the homeless problem. PUJ activist Nibs Stroup said, "They raised $142 million for Underground Atlanta, and they won't raise $4 million for the homeless. We are not asking for a whole lot."[217] An activist who was previously homeless, Eddie Torres, added, "They don't want to help because it's not convenient to Atlanta." Joe Martin, a senior advisor to Mayor Jackson, responded, "Every business person in this town realizes there is a need for affordable housing."[218]

Houston critiqued the lack of progress on SRO development in a document entitled "Thus Saith The Lord of Housing: 'You're Too Slow With the SROs.'" He wryly stated in the opening sentence, "Slow is an understatement."[219] Houston charged that even though PUJ's desire for affordable housing had a prophetic message, the number of homeless people accelerated at an unprecedented rate, while the production of affordable housing proceeded at a snail's pace. Houston criticized Mayor Jackson for not fulfilling his promise, and he harangued the Atlanta banking community, charging them with setting a "scenario of resistance." Additionally, he called out the Atlanta corporate community for ever-so-slowly committing to the Atlanta Housing Equity Fund, which he described as "not a charity" because there would be a "15-20 percent profit that local corporations could make as a result of the funding being used for affordable multi-family and SRO production."[220]

Roughly 20 to 25 corporations had been approached within the previous two years to pledge $250,000 to the fund, but contributions were sparse. The Atlanta Housing Equity Fund had been set up and had pledges totaling $3.5 million from ten companies including BankSouth, Delta Air Lines, First Union, Georgia Pacific, Home Depot, NationsBank, Trust Company, and Wachovia.[221] What motivated them to donate, however, was that the

Maryland-based Enterprise Social Investment Corporation said it would withdraw its $1 million match unless Atlanta businesses pledged at least $2 million by the end of 1991.[222]

CHAPTER TWELVE
WELCOME HOUSE

Shortly after the June 1990 occupation of the Imperial Hotel, arrangements were put in motion to replace the Welcome House shelter with a Welcome House SRO. At the end of August, approximately 130 people had been staying at the 200-bed Welcome House facility. Churches visited the shelter for weekly Bible study and Grady Hospital offered health screenings. Residents showered in shifts in the makeshift environs. In August, Shirley Franklin, a liaison to Welcome House, was impressed with the facility. She also indicated that it provided a model for the 3,500 units of SRO housing Mayor Jackson had proposed, especially because homeless people were in leadership positions at the shelter.[223] Franklin's concept of homeless self-empowerment was called into question in December when the city removed Bill Jones from his post as director of the shelter. Jones, an Executive Committee member and negotiator during the Imperial occupation, was expelled under controversial circumstances, and the ensuing realignment of power significantly weakened homeless leaders' control of the shelter.[224] Additionally, it was reported that the shelter had been "mired in internal squabbles."[225]

By late 1991, a host of problems had stalled the SRO project including financing, land issues, bad weather, politics, and an environmental cleanup resulting from an old sewer leak. Construction was delayed for a month shortly after the groundbreaking ceremony when it was discovered that a 100-year-old abandoned sewer had contaminated the soil on the proposed site, which was in an industrial warehouse area. It cost $150,000 to haul out the bad soil and the two industrial oil tanks that were discovered there. The city agreed to reimburse PRI (the non-profit company that would operate the facility) for the cost of environmental cleanup.[226]

In January 1992, events took a positive turn when a $1.4 million loan was approved for the project.[227] Anita Beaty called the loan "one of the most important things to ever happen in housing in the city. This Welcome House project is a symbol as much as a reality for the homeless people."[228] Charles S. Scheid, the executive director of the consortium of the ten largest lenders in metro Atlanta, indicated that the group had committed to construction. "The mayor made a promise, and that promise is finally going to be a reality," he said.[229] Lyn May, a spokesperson for Mayor Jackson, reported, "The Mayor is very encouraged by the letter of commitment, and he looks forward to the ultimate completion of the project."[230]

Bruce Gunter, president of PRI, responded: "I want to laud the Downtown banking community on this one . . . This is a breakthrough."[231] Gunter's Christian faith motivated him to create affordable housing. A member of Atlanta's St. Luke's Episcopal Church, Gunter was no stranger to witnessing poverty, homelessness, and suffering. "I'm a Christian," he said, "As I understand my faith, it calls me – it commands me, actually, to look after my neighbor and to tend to those who are hungry and naked. It's a radical gospel that calls us to do these things. And it's an order, not a suggestion, if you take it seriously."[232]

From Shelter to SRO

For the city's homeless activists, housing officials, bankers, and developers, building the Welcome House SRO was an exhausting lesson in creating affordable housing at a time when federal resources had dried up and municipal governments were strapped for cash. "It's absolutely the hardest thing I've ever done in my life," claimed Mike Griffin of PRI. "We had to hold people's hands every step of the way, and we had to pull teeth for every piece of financing we got," he added.[233]

Gunter said that even with the mayor's support for the project they still encountered a lot of difficulties. With nine layers of financing, the funding was complex. Additionally, because there were so few SROs recently developed in Atlanta, banks were skeptical about loaning money for the project.[234] Funding streams included private debt, subsidies, tax credits, loans, grants, and a trust fund. In addition to pulling in financial backing from nine banks in a local lending consortium, there were other agencies involved in the funding process: the Enterprise Social Investment Corporation, Federal Home Loan Bank, Georgia Housing Finance Authority, Metropolitan Atlanta Community Foundation, and the City of Atlanta.[235]

Ray Kuniansky, a banker affiliated with the project, revealed that one problem was that banks were trying to use conventional financing even though they did not have much experience with underwriting this kind of project. As a result, they had to do a lot of pioneering work. A significant problem was projected cash flow: the developer was targeting residents who could pay seven dollars a night, but this created a gap between income and expenses for the mortgage. Kuniansky added that it became obvious that multiple sources of funding were needed if the project was to be completed.[236] These sources were found, but according to Stan Goldsboro, a specialist with the Georgia Housing Finance Authority, the variety of funding sources caused the project to be in a constant state of flux. He described it as a dynamic process for a number of years. Every time a new source of funding was added, the rules changed. "Every source was trying to protect their part of the action," Goldsboro said, and each had their own underwriting requirements. Financial delays in the closing of the loans, for example, caused construction to be halted in June of 1992. After agreements were reached, construction resumed in July.[237]

There were also political issues that had to be worked out before construction was completed. Like the proposed SRO site in Lake Claire, acceptance was potentially tenuous. Goldsboro explained that the concept had to be accepted politically: "This is in the downtown area. It may not be the most prime land, but anything in the downtown area tends to have certain perceptions by the business community. There had to be mutual education on how it was going to be managed and what type of impact, socially speaking, this type of a facility would have on an area so close to downtown. It took a while to reach comfort levels acceptable to all parties involved."[238]

Bradfield, Richards and Associates designed the brick and stucco Welcome House. Richard Bradfield, principal architect, had years of experience designing low-income housing, and he had recently traveled to San Diego to study SRO development there. Early in the planning stages, Bill Jones and other Welcome House shelter residents offered input into the

Welcome House, 2013. Photo by author.

design and rent structure of the SRO. H.J. Russell Construction Company built Welcome House. They had recently completed the Stratford Inn, so they had experience with SRO construction.[239]

The grand opening of Welcome House was December 18, 1992, eighteen months after the Imperial Hotel occupation. The final location was 234 Memorial Drive at the intersection of Pryor Street in the South Central Business District, three blocks south of city hall. The list of speakers at the ribbon-cutting ceremony and open house included Bruce Gunter and Mike Griffin from PRI, Congressperson John Lewis, and Rev. Timothy McDonald.[240] Mayor Jackson presided over the ceremonies. At the event, Gunter coyly showed Jackson a photo of the threatening banner he and the others had hung from the Imperial's high window in September 1991 ("Dear Maynard, Back to the Imperial? Keep Your Promise") without revealing who was responsible for it. Jackson demonstrated a sense of humor about the media-savvy action.[241]

On December 31, 1992, Welcome House SRO opened for tenants as a residential SRO community for working, low-income individuals. Tenants paid seven to nine dollars per night for a 100-square-foot carpeted room equipped with a twin-sized bed, dresser, desk, chair, refrigerator, lavatory, and sink. Laundry, bathroom, lounge, and kitchen facilities were shared. There were 163 single rooms and 46 double rooms. Residents signed six-month leases, paid a twenty dollar application fee, a five dollar phone deposit, and the first week's rent. If applicants could not show proof of employment or some prior rental history, they were required to undergo six months of counseling services.[242]

PRI's philosophical perspective on affordable housing was grounded in the notion of having high quality, social service-enriched environments for people on the margins; consequently, they believed that residents should be offered direct access to on-site or nearby social services.[243] PRI's affordable housing model fit the definition of supportive housing endorsed by the Corporation for Supportive Housing, that understands that low-income (or no-income) residents face complex challenges. Supportive services, they insist, are designed to improve residents' mental, physical, and economic health so they may live more stable, autonomous, productive, and dignified lives.[244]

Support services at Welcome House included a full-time, on-site social services manager who worked with tenants to assist them with services such as counseling, transportation, job training, health treatment, food acquisition, and computer literacy. Welcome House was Georgia's first Shelter Plus Care site, a part of HUD's Supportive Housing Program. Shelter Plus Care targeted formerly homeless people and others at risk of homelessness. Fifty units at Welcome House were allocated to this program.

Mayor Jackson called the $3.3 million building an "amazing victory" that helped fulfill part of his promise to build 3,500 units of housing for the homeless.[245] Stan Goldsboro believed the next SRO would be easier to build: "You have a lot of different homeless groups vying for involvement. You got a lot of players, a lot of stakeholders, but now that we've gotten this one under our belt, the next one can become a little easier. We have a model now, and we brought people to the same table and achieved comfort levels."[246]

Goldsboro described Welcome House as a monument to a lot of people's hard work. Gunter agreed: "Right now, I couldn't be more pleased. People are happy with the appearance of the building. We are happy with the lease . . . happy with the house rules. We even ended up with $30,000 in donated landscaping plants. It's going well right now."[247]

Despite all of the positive features of Welcome House, potential problems were soon detected. Homeless person Winston Russell had mixed feelings about Welcome House. Winston was a participant in the Imperial Hotel occupation, and he questioned the lasting value of that event. "Did we accomplish anything?" he asked. "In a sense, yes, and in a sense, no," he said. "I'm glad it's here, but it's not really for homeless people so it didn't really accomplish what we were trying to do."[248] Jon Abercrombie, executive director of FCS Urban Ministries, stated, "One of the challenges is that the SROs have to pay their own way, and no one has been able to get the numbers down low enough for those who are living out there on the streets."[248] He added, "Until we can subsidize folks' rents to lower the costs, we are still missing folks at the bottom end of the economic ladder." Houston Wheeler acknowledged the affordability problem when he pointed out that most of the units rented for sixty-nine dollars per week, which was twenty dollars higher than PUJ and the Welcome House Executive Committee advocated for.[250]

Jimmy Lightfoot had been sleeping nights under a highway overpass nearby, and he did not think that he would qualify to live at Welcome House. He was unable to secure proper identification and he did not have a steady income from the labor pools where he worked. "If I was living there and couldn't pay my rent, they would kick me out," he remarked. In a dejected tone he added, "I guess I'll just say a prayer, stay up under my bridge and try to survive."[251]

CHAPTER THIRTEEN
OLYMPIC DIVERSIONS

In addition to the problems encountered by financing, political will, and the geography of SRO development, another issue diverted attention from affordable housing development – the upcoming 1996 Olympics. In September 1990, Atlanta learned that it would host the 1996 Olympic Games. By late 1992, planning was in full tilt. The improvements that the city wanted to make to prepare for the Olympics were estimated at nearly $700 million. The city Planning Bureau had an ambitious wish list and they worked to secure local, state, and national funds. Hoped-for projects included improvements in streetscapes, public transportation, and parks. [252] In the ensuing years, Olympic zeal overshadowed affordable housing development.

Concern grew as Olympic planning unfolded. For starters, The Atlanta Committee for the Olympic Games did not disclose much information to the public, and some people were disturbed by the secrecy of the Olympic bid package. Skeptics also questioned the financial, societal, environmental, and individual human effects of hosting the Olympics. They worried about how the Games would affect Atlanta's poor and dispossessed people during a time of decreasing affordable housing, declining incomes, and diminishing federal assistance. [253]

There was a concerted effort by the city to remove "undesirables" from public view in downtown Atlanta. A report noted: "By the 1996 Olympic Games, Atlanta may well make the claim that there are no homeless people in the city – because most will be in jail."[254] Comments like this were responses to city hall's increasing measures to control public space. For example, in July 1991 the Atlanta city council had passed a set of ordinances sponsored by the

Public Safety Committee. For critics, these "anti-poor" or "anti-panhandling" ordinances criminalized Atlanta's homeless populations. The ordinances made it unlawful to:

1. Enter a vacant building

2. Enter onto a parking lot unless the person's car is parked there or the person has lawful business on the property

3. Beg or solicit alms (by spoken, written, or printed word or other method) by accosting another or by forcing oneself upon the company of another[255]

Another ordinance made it unlawful to lie down on a public park bench. The apparent aim of these ordinances was to create "sanitized corridors," "hospitality zones," and "vagrant-free zones" for the Olympics.

People for Urban Justice was appalled. Carol Schlicksup stated, "This is a city that believes in hiding its poor. The Olympics are going to devastate the poor communities."[256] It was feared that the Olympics would open the gateway for a repeat of what happened during the 1988 Democratic National Convention, when Atlanta police removed homeless people from the streets to present a better image of the city.[257]

Atlanta musician Joyce Brookshire captured the thrust of people's concern in her song "What Will We Do With the Homeless (When the Olympics Come to Town)?" Comprised of three verses and a chorus, the lyrics voiced Brookshire's fear of economic segregation while suggesting that affordable housing was a solution to homelessness:

Verse 1:

When the world comes to Atlanta
Where will the homeless be
Will we march them to Oklahoma
Like we did with the Cherokee
Will we shove them into alleys
Dare them to show their face
Or make them a major Olympic event
How 'bout a homeless race

Chorus:

Oh, what will we do with the homeless
When the Olympics come to town
What will we do with the homeless

> Hide them Underground,
> Oh, what will we do with the homeless,
> We cannot allow them to roam
> What will we do with the homeless
> Why don't we find them a home[258]

Drawing from southern cultural icons, Brookshire surmises in the final verse that if affordable housing was provided, then Atlanta could present an honest portrait during the Olympics: "We'll show them our closets and corners / No homeless folk will they find / Then we'll all share a Coke and a peach pie / And have an Olympic good time."

Brookshire wrote the song in 1990 when she heard the announcement that Atlanta would host the 1996 Olympics. In 1994, Brookshire said, "Four years later there is still no clearcut answer to my question. However, new ordinances have been written by the Atlanta City Council, establishing a Hospitality Zone, where the homeless are strongly urged not to be . . . Very little has been done by the city to create low-income housing for the homeless."[259] In 1993, Brookshire sang the song to Mayor Jackson. "He was not amused," she revealed.[260]

The Metro Atlanta Task Force for the Homeless released a study in 1993 that showed a correlation between the staging of conventions and the arrests of homeless people. Police sweeps were being used to clear the streets before major downtown conventions. The task force pointed out that the high cost of arresting and detaining homeless people for minor statutes and homeless ordinances prevented the city from supporting the creation of affordable housing, jobs, and services. The task force estimated the city was spending between $300,000 and $500,000 per year to incarcerate homeless people.[261]

Broken Promises

Judging by the pace of affordable housing production since the Imperial occupation, there was no way that the promise of 3,500 units could be met by 1994. Houston Wheeler calculated that at the current rate of roughly 100 spaces per year, it would take 35 years to complete the promise. Three housing sites that were targeted for specific populations (such as tenants with mental or physical health issues) were not available for general working poor and homeless individuals and families. Other sites targeted for future development had no solid financial backing. And by putting the Welcome House SRO on land previously used for an emergency shelter, the city lost 125 emergency shelter beds that were unlikely to be replaced.[262]

Houston summed up his thoughts about the progress of affordable housing development since the occupation: "There is absolutely no way the promises of the Memorandum of Understanding signed by Mayor Jackson on July 3, 1990, can be met. The total number of new and affordable SRO spaces completed since the signing of the Memorandum totals 209. The promise was to have 1,000 of the 3,500 units completed during the first year. At the current rate of about 100 new spaces per year, it will take 10 years or until the year 2000 to complete the first 1,000 and 35 years, or the year 2025 to complete the promised 3,500 units."[263]

Time to Renegotiate the Memorandum of Understanding

PUJ devised a strategy to prod Mayor Jackson to move faster on SRO development. On December 1, 1992, Frances Pauley wrote a letter to Mayor Jackson and other political and business leaders requesting that he renegotiate the Memorandum of Understanding that he had signed in July of 1990. She outlined three reasons for the necessity to renegotiate: financing was not materializing, current SROs were not addressing the core homeless population, and the Memorandum of Understanding had been written before it was announced that Atlanta would host the 1996 Olympics.[264]

It was projected that roughly 15,000 to 20,000 homeless people would be living in Atlanta by 1996. While this enraged PUJ, they also used it as leverage. Pauley indicated that 10,000 units of SRO housing (6,500 more than proposed in the Memorandum of Understanding) would be needed by 1996 to prevent Atlanta from being embarrassed by human rights violations as homeless people wandered the streets during the Olympics.[265]

In her letter, Pauley also prompted Mayor Jackson to develop housing for seven to eight dollars a night, a rate that low-wage workers could afford, especially those who worked in labor pools. She urged Jackson to curtail criminalization of homelessness and to renew his commitment to house homeless people. She pointed out that "Hutsville," a homeless encampment under the viaduct at the intersection of Martin Luther King Boulevard and

Techwood Street, was clear evidence of the dearth of affordable housing for Atlanta's poor population. In closing, Pauley warned, "If negotiations do not take place or an agreement is not reached, People for Urban Justice will take other steps to dramatize the need for affordable housing."[266]

A Homeless Manifesto

PUJ also created the "Atlanta Homeless Manifesto 1993 Agreement." Pauley included a draft of the manifesto in her December 1, 1992, letter to Mayor Jackson and other political and business leaders. This document was an agreement in principle that civic and business leaders would take specific steps to finance the production of 10,000 units of affordable housing. More specifically, it stated that the participants would agree to collaborate in public/private partnerships while adhering to these general principles:

- To call upon the religious leaders of Atlanta to pray and preach each Sabbath that homelessness is a human rights violation and an injustice upon homeless persons and the entire Atlanta community;

- To call upon the religious, business, and government leaders of Atlanta to pray and preach each Sabbath for the financing and production of affordable housing for homeless persons in Atlanta;

- That 10,000 homeless persons will be permanently housed by the new construction of 3,500 units and the rehabilitation of 6,500 existing units;

- That the mayor, Atlanta City Council, Fulton County Commission, Central Atlanta Progress, and the Atlanta Project will work in partnership and commit to have 10,000 affordable housing units for homeless persons financed and produced by the winter of 1996 (3,500 new construction, 6,500 rehab of existing units);

- That these SROs and affordable housing for homeless persons will be located equally in each city council district of the city of Atlanta which means at least 500 units in each district;

• That the financing of these SROs and affordable housing for homeless persons will be worked out on a project by project basis using the following basic formula: $16,000 - $18,000 per unit, $160-$180 million [overall]; 1/3 debt through local banks [as a fulfillment of their community reinvestment act responsibility]; 1/3 tax credits through the Atlanta Housing Equity Fund; 1/3 grants from governments, foundations, religious institutions, and individuals.[267]

In February 1993, Houston Wheeler sent a letter to Mayor Jackson and other political and business leaders reminding them that PUJ had asked the city to renegotiate the Memorandum of Understanding. He emphasized that affordable housing projects were underfunded while other projects flourished:

While the city of Atlanta has identified housing the homeless as its number one priority, the financing of this goal has not sufficiently happened, nor will it happen without a public/private partnership from governments, foundations, local banks, and tax credits. Other priorities get financed but not housing the homeless. Local governments and the business community figure out ways to fund stadiums and infrastructure projects, but not to house its poorest citizens. The image portrayed is that Atlanta cares more about housing the rich than housing the poor – Atlanta cares more about Super Bowls and Olympic events than about homeless African American men who fill Atlanta's jails. The jails in Atlanta and Fulton County reveal Atlanta's real housing policy.[268]

Houston added that when PUJ attorney Brian Spears asked representatives gathered at a January 29, 1993, meeting at Central Atlanta Progress if they wished to negotiate the Atlanta Homeless Manifesto 1993 Agreement, there was no response. Wheeler noted that PUJ interpreted this silence as a decision not to renegotiate the document, and he warned, "As we said in our previous correspondence to you, if negotiations do not take place or if an agreement is not reached, PUJ will take steps to dramatize the need for affordable housing for homeless persons."

Banks and Protests

PUJ also turned its attention to banks. They notified banks that they must expedite financing for affordable housing or face negative publicity. In September 1993, under the threat of demonstrations outside their headquarters, executives from Trust Company Bank of Georgia met with PUJ representatives. At this point, Atlanta banks were already being scrutinized for their discriminatory home-lending practices as a result of the 1988 Pulitzer-winning investigative newspaper series "The Color of Money," so they were sensitive to criticism and responsive to discussion.[269] PUJ had studied lending laws, and they pushed banks to honor their requirements to finance affordable housing. They argued that the banks should be held accountable for financing affordable housing and that Trust Company Bank and other Atlanta banks had failed to meet that responsibility.[270]

Houston explained, "We're tired of meeting for the sake of meeting. We want some concrete action by the banking industry."[271] Trust Company Bank was the first to get PUJ's attention because it was the only bank to positively respond to their Pre-Olympic Plan for Housing Homeless Persons in Atlanta. Trust Company Bank said in a letter that PUJ was reasonable in its basic affordable housing financing formula of one-third each from tax credits, direct subsidies, and bank financing. Houston insisted that PUJ would use the tactic of threatened demonstrations to get other banks to negotiate.[272]

A Pre-Olympic Plan for Affordable Housing

PUJ published a collection of material aiming to remind leaders and residents of the need for affordable housing. Titled "A Pre-Olympic Plan for Housing Homeless Persons in Atlanta," the document asserted that the "Beloved Atlanta Community" would emerge when homeless and poor people were decently housed.[273] While acknowledging Atlanta's monumental achievements, PUJ decried the abject poverty and suffering of Atlanta's homeless and public housing residents while challenging leadership to address affordable housing and community reinvestment issues. Their call was urgent: the fabric of democracy depended upon all people being decently housed.[274]

Houston Wheeler's sermon, "Fulfilling the Imperial Hotel Promise," pointed out that although Mayor Jackson promised affordable housing, the Olympic preparations destroyed that promise. He believed that the banks and government were so keyed up over the Olympics that it was like a runaway steamroller. He claimed: "The Imperial Hotel Promise was a covenant to reinvest in affordable housing for homeless persons. Instead, with the Olympic Games, we've gotten nuisance ordinances . . . So, instead of investing to fulfill the . . . promise, the banks, governments, and foundations are diverting their funding toward pro-Olympic projects. The net effect . . . causes the continued and increased harassment and oppression of homeless persons in Atlanta. By rejecting the promise, the pharaohs of Atlanta are putting their blessing on the displacement of homeless persons."[275]

A Five-Point Proposal

In another strategy, PUJ devised a "Five-Point Proposal," the name referencing Five Points, a core area of the city and the central hub of Atlanta's rapid rail and bus system. The message was directed to Mayor Jackson and city council candidates, the elected officials who, if elected, would wield power to eliminate or reduce a range of problems facing Atlanta's homeless people. PUJ urged them to focus their attention on five points:

1. To support PUJ's Pre-Olympic Plan for Housing Homeless Persons in Atlanta (10,000 units/beds in 10 years with financing from banks, tax credits, and grants from government and foundations)

2. To expand the city's shelter beds by 1,000

3. To repeal nuisance ordinances such as Vagrant Free Zone laws

4. To provide public toilets

5. To enforce the city's labor pool ordinance, which would guarantee workers' rights[276]

In 1994, Mayor Jackson's third term ended. The Imperial Hotel had fallen into foreclosure, it remained vacant, and it was an eyesore. But it was on the National Historical Register, so could not be torn down. In May 1994, the current owner, Jamestown Properties, petitioned to wrap the building in a gigantic advertising mural during the 1996 Olympics to raise revenue to pay for eventual restoration, but the city did not approve the proposal.[277]

In 1995, when Mayor Bill Campbell took office, PUJ's affordable housing advocacy continued. On August 17, 1995, Houston wrote to Wit Carson, chairman of the Georgia Housing Finance Authority, and copied the letter to Mayor Campbell and Governor Zell Miller. He urged Mr. Carson to do what he could to make sure PRI would get the tax credits it needed to renovate the Imperial Hotel. He asked, "When the Olympics come to our city next summer, where will the homeless sleep?" Wheeler responded to his own question: "The Imperial Hotel seems as good a place as any – renovation or no renovation," and added, "If PRI doesn't get its tax credits, we'll just raise a few dollars for some [portable toilets] and take it over again. Maybe a second takeover will get through."[278]

CHAPTER FOURTEEN

IMPERIAL HOTEL RESURRECTION(S)

In 1995, three years after PRI completed Welcome House, they turned their attention to the Imperial Hotel. Bruce Gunter approached Mayor Bill Campbell, informing him about PRI's desire to assemble multiple-layer financing to create an SRO at the Imperial that would be mixed-income housing.[279]

PRI asked the city for a $1 million loan to purchase the building. They charged that it would be a showcase of affordable housing at a time when this kind of housing was on the decline. Some of the units would be rented to people who were formerly homeless; other units would be rented to people who earned less than $20,000 a year; some units would be set aside for market-rate renters.[280] Similar to Welcome House, on-site services would be provided for tenants. Housing Commissioner Carl Hartrampf persuaded Mayor Bill Campbell to authorize the $1 million city loan.[281]

Gunter described the Imperial purchase and its subsequent renovation as an incredibly complex project. Financing from every level of government and five banks was involved as they renovated the building for modern use while retaining historical architectural features, including the original "I.H." insignia on the molding. Even though the political establishment was behind the project, prior to closing the purchasing deal, PRI had to demonstrate that they had the necessary $10 million in renovation funds fully committed to them. The final piece of funding was a $500,000 contract to lease the building to the Atlanta Committee for the Olympic Games (ACOG), who wanted the building refurbished for aesthetic reasons but also because they were interested in housing international journalists there during the

Left: The lobby of the Imperial Hotel during the 1996 renovation. Photo courtesy of Progressive Redevelopment.

Right: The lobby of the The Imperial on Peachtree after the 1996 renovation of the Imperial Hotel. Photo courtesy of Progressive Redevelopment.

Games.[282] A condition of the contract was that PRI had to guarantee on-time completion of the project.

A Monday deadline rapidly approached for the final paperwork to be settled. On the Friday evening prior to that Monday, ACOG called PRI indicating that they were no longer interested in the contract. PRI had "bet the ranch" on the Imperial purchase and renovation, so ACOG's announcement was a serious blow to their entire portfolio of affordable housing. Gunter realized the meaning of ACOG's decision: he responded by communicating that if they would not honor their commitment, then 100 homeless people would be in their lobby Monday morning. The next day Gunter was summoned to ACOG's office. After Gunter received what he called a "blistering lecture," the contract was signed, the deal was done, and PRI would remain open to do the renovation and build affordable housing.[283]

PRI purchased the building in March 1995 for $970,000 from Jamestown Properties. In addition to the $1 million loan from the city of Atlanta, a federal low-income tax credit was a significant part of the financing. The tax credit provided equity so that individuals could invest in the project for tax credits. The non-profit Corporation for Supportive Housing also played a key role in financing the project. Overall, over ten sources of public and private financing were used to renovate the hotel. PRI secured a $1.75 million loan from Wachovia, NationsBank, and SunTrust. The City of Atlanta, the Georgia Department of Community Affairs, and the State Housing Trust Fund for the Homeless provided more than $2 million. The Federal Home Loan Bank and the Atlanta Neighborhood Development Partnership financed a portion of the construction loan.

Fannie Mae and Standard Mortgage provided permanent financing. Federal historic preservation tax credits tallying $4.5 million were also part of the multi-layered financing for the project.[284]

With funding in place, PRI aimed to build permanent, affordable, and supportive housing, despite opposition from several nearby businesses. Their plans soon became more detailed: the building would have one-third of the rooms available for formerly homeless people enrolled in job training or work programs. Other rooms would be designated for "employed mentally impaired or disabled people who qualify for supportive housing with rents as low as $425 a month."[285] The remaining units would be filled with downtown workers earning less than $21,000 a year.[286] There were expected to be 74 efficiency apartments and 46 one-bedroom apartments.

Dignitaries gathered December 20, 1995, to announce commencement of the renovation. By mid-January, workers had already gutted the structure.[287] Next, Smith Dalia Architects and the construction team labored to create a modern, comfortable living space while retaining historic features, such as rebuilding the front porch, reconditioning the bay windows, reproducing woodwork, and restoring the lobby to its "original grandeur."[288] Workers were "turn[ing] the great stone shell into a warm abode for those who need it the most: the homeless."[289] Journalist S.A. Reid reported that even though exotic dancers and other unbecoming activity had overshadowed the hotel's pedigree, it was getting a second life.[290] "The homeless aren't the only winners in this situation," said Gunter. "The entire city of Atlanta will benefit from this rare historic jewel restored to its former splendor."[291]

The original estimate for the renovation was $6 million. By the

The front of the Imperial Hotel before the 1996 renovation. Photo courtesy of Progressive Redevelopment.

time construction was completed, the cost was $9.5 million. The increase was partly due to skyrocketing construction costs during the Olympic building era, but it was also because union labor was used on the project.[292]

Grand Opening

The SRO opened as The Imperial on Peachtree in December 1996. At the December 18 grand opening ceremony, people rejoiced at the beauty of the building and the promise it held for future tenants. Bankers, politicians, and Mayor Campbell mingled with homeless people. Bruce Gunter called the grand opening a "remarkable celebration of a resurrection story." He believed the project demonstrated that "people of good will and strong faith could make a difference." He was, it seems, referring not only to the courageous PUJ activists and homeless people who put their bodies on the line to demonstrate the urgent need for affordable housing, but also to the people who committed their working lives to helping create a Beloved Community in Atlanta.[293]

The front of The Imperial on Peachtree after the 1996 renovation of the Imperial Hotel. Photo courtesy of the Open Door Community via Gay Construction Co.

At the ceremony, over 20 partners and contributors were listed in the program brochure. Mike Griffin offered the welcome remarks. Rev. Samuel Matthews of First United Methodist Church gave the invocation. Gunter provided the introduction and "Presentation to the City." Mayor Bill Campbell addressed the gathering. Eduard Loring delivered a "thunderous" sermon along with a history of the hotel occupation. LaVone Griffin, executive director of Theatrical Visionaries, and a former tenant of SRO housing, provided a "street theater" vignette of a play he had co-written with Atlanta playwright Rebecca Ransom. The original play, "Stormy Road Onward" (the acronym for the performance was a

The side of the Imperial Hotel before completion of the 1996 renovation. Photo courtesy of Progressive Redevelopment.

word play on Single-Room-Occupancy), explored the trials and triumphs of people experiencing housing and employment difficulties, and it was based on interviews with homeless people and those living in transitional housing. Elise Witt, the Atlanta musician and educator who had joined protesters inside the hotel during the occupation, sang. Woody Bartlett, program director of the Corporation for Supportive Housing, gave closing remarks. Rev. Stephen Churchwell of Sacred Heart Church provided the Benediction. A lunch was served and tours of the historic restoration and "spectacular" views were encouraged.[294] Open Door Community resident Gladys Rustay called the vista from the upper floors "million-dollar views."

At the end of December, 1996, 73 percent of the units were leased. PRI expected that by the end of March 1997 there would be 100 percent occupancy.[295] There were 120 rooms: 74 efficiency apartments and 46 one-bedroom apartments. The efficiency apartments were 245 square feet; the one-bedroom apartments were 375 square feet. Features included 24-hour front desk service and controlled access for safety, a laundry facility, a library, a conference room, a dining room, a common kitchen, office space, decorator carpets, cable TV, and elevators. Utilities were included in the price of the room.[296] An advertisement proclaimed: "If you're looking for a better way of living *and* intown convenience, come to The Imperial on Peachtree. Formerly known as the Imperial Hotel, this apartment community is rich in history, yet offers many of today's most wanted features. So, if you want quality housing and earn less than $21,900 a year, call now. It may be your first step toward an affordable Peachtree Street address!"[297]

The side of The Imperial on Peachtree after the 1996 renovation of the Imperial Hotel. Photo courtesy of Progressive Redevelopment.

Mercy Mobile, an affiliate of St. Joseph's Mercy Care Services, provided on-site support for tenants. Services included resources for and assistance with addiction recovery, physical disabilities, mental health issues, crisis intervention, employment, and community and civic engagement.

Units were restricted to individuals who earned no more than 60 percent of Atlanta's median income.[298] Rents ranged from $425 to $513 a month.[299] The target population for this income group was downtown workers and others such as formerly homeless or near homeless people with special needs who could not afford market rate rent.[300] Thirty-five units were set aside for people who were formerly homeless with special needs; this provided a place for those who were caught between homelessness and being able to afford market-rate rent in a traditional apartment.[301] More than half of the units were available for residents who qualified for Section 8 Housing (federal rent subsidy program), so it was a public and private partnership, and that meant tenants paid only a portion of the rent while the federal government covered the balance.[302]

Mike Griffin revealed that PRI's "magic" was to use public subsidies to leverage private financing.[303] State Senator Nan Orrock called the opening of the affordable housing units a miracle. Orrock had worked at the state level to get funds for the restoration. She believed that the renovated building would be especially meaningful for homeless people because they themselves made it happen.[304] Mayor Bill Campbell asserted that the renovation was a symbol for the city's compassion.[305] A newspaper headline announced: "Imperial's Majesty Restored."[306] Another proclaimed: "Down-Home Rent for Uptown

Living."[307] Anita Beaty called the renovation a "victory for homeless people, their advocates, service providers and developers, who understand that the best way to provide for the homeless is to collaborate on housing."[308] Gunter, who clearly understood the virtues of collaboration, exclaimed, "Partnership is the overwhelming theme here . . . So many institutions came together to make this thing possible."[309]

Amid the celebratory mood, however, Gunter cautioned, "We still have poor people in Atlanta that still don't have housing. That's unfortunate . . . [but] it's nice to get this one off our backs."[310]

Imperial residents welcomed the building's affordable rent and amenities. Some viewed the residence as a chance for a new start in life. Larry Clark, a resident who had previously lived in substandard housing, exclaimed, "When I found The Imperial, a change came – a miracle happened."[311] Clark worked part-time in nursing and paid 30 percent of his salary toward rent at the Imperial; the remaining balance was subsidized by the government. He reflected, "I was in a very depressed stage of my life when I found out about The Imperial . . . In less than a year, I've been able to get myself back on focus. Because I found this place, I've been able to pull myself back together."

Gladys Rustay noted that a former Open Door resident, Karen Thomas, rented an apartment at the newly-renovated Imperial. "It's a sad story," Gladys recalled: "She was so anxious to get in. She had cancer. She was going to have all the women of the Open Door come down and see her house and she was going to have tea. A female police officer helped her get furniture

Interior of an apartment in The Imperial on Peachtree after the 1996 renovation of the Imperial Hotel. Photo courtesy of the Open Door Community via Gay Construction Co.

and that was just great. Her doctor said she had lung cancer, but she denied having it. She was found by her friends on the floor of the apartment. She was at the Imperial for a short time, not more than a month." In a 1997 *Hospitality* article about the re-opening of the Imperial Hotel, Stacia Brown remembered that Karen was excited about having her own kitchen and her own space.[312] The Open Door Community has dedicated a room to her.

Spirituality in a Pinstripe Suit

Bruce Gunter called the homeless problem a "business challenge." He faulted the business community for not understanding that helping to find permanent solutions to the homeless problem would be far less costly to them in the long term than ignoring the problem. According to the city of Atlanta's Human Services Department, by late 1996, there were 3,500 shelter beds and an average of 10,000 homeless people on any given night in Atlanta. Gunter was well aware of those numbers and the pain associated with them.[313]

Gunter reasoned that his pinstripe suit is his most important tool in building homes for homeless and working poor people. It is an essential tool of his trade: "I'm in pinstripes because when you raise money – even for homeless people and poor people – you have to go to banks . . . The resource communities need to have confidence and comfort with you, so I never leave the pinstripes behind."

Gunter believes that homelessness and poverty are not moral choices people make, but rather the product of economic factors. He blamed the disappearance of decent-paying blue-collar jobs as a significant factor contributing to poverty and homelessness. Gunter also asserted that problems with mental or physical health are key factors that lead some people to homelessness and poverty, especially when they lack a stable social network. Gunter preferred to see homeless people *as* people: "We tend to see them as *The Homeless* [emphasis added] – as though they are just one big mass of people with all kinds of problems. But we overlook the fact that each homeless person is an individual tragedy and is entitled to dignity and compassion."[314]

Even though some SRO and affordable housing units were created in the years following the Imperial Hotel occupation, at least one reason why more units were not created was because financing low-income housing construction and renovation was extremely complex. Gunter explained: "Financing low-income housing can be as complicated a real-estate transaction as there is. You are mixing public sector financing – government programs with the attendant red tape together with bank loans and syndicated equity. It's like seeing sausage made – you don't want to know how it's done." Gunter considered it a "cruel paradox" that, strikingly, the lower the income, the more complicated the deals: "They are fiendishly complicated. That's one reason not much is done. In addition to limited funding and the politics, there are not enough people with skills to put these things together."[315]

With a business background and a master's degree in business administration specializing in finance, Gunter discovered that his knowledge and skills were highly valued among "goodhearted" social justice advocates who were passionate about improving poor people's lives. Not only did Gunter realize that his work was enjoyable and satisfying, he also discovered that through developing affordable housing he found his voice. He also learned that understanding politics is as important as knowing economics: "You have to know when to duck, when to play to the moral card, when to combat the stereotypes."[316]

As a developer, PRI bought land or a building, financed it, renovated it, and moved people into it. They frequently remained as the owners of the building. Gunter acknowledged the resistance PRI sometimes faced when developing housing for low-income people: "Nobody, in any neighborhood, ever says, 'Great, let's do some low-income housing.' That's part of what we have to overcome. And the way we overcome that is to do well. Well-built, well-run affordable housing can be a good neighbor – as it should be."[317]

When PRI purchased the Imperial in 1995 it was a vacant and dreary hulk. It was a symbol of downtown's decline, a casualty of central city deterioration. It was a depressed market at that time, so the building was not developed. Gunter contended that the city was not doing much about rising homelessness so a determined band of activists with desperation and religious conviction took it upon themselves to do something about it: the 1990 Imperial Hotel action and occupation.[318] The transformation of the hotel into affordable housing six years later was a direct result of PUJ's sixteen-day peaceful protest.

The Imperial on Peachtree was an award-winning renovation. In 1997, the *Atlanta Business Chronicle* voted it "Best in Atlanta Real Estate" in rehabilitation.[319] It also won an Atlanta Urban Design Award, a Georgia

Association of General Contractors award, and a Georgia AIA Sustainable Design award.[320] After PRI renovated the hotel, they characterized it as the "grand dame" with her luster restored.[321] They also claimed that The Imperial on Peachtree was "Atlanta's finest example of supportive housing, being both a good neighbor and a good home to over 120 individuals, many of whom would be on the streets were it not for the Imperial's affordable rents and extensive support services."[322]

Hard Times at the Imperial

For nearly thirteen years The Imperial on Peachtree was an example of successful affordable and supportive housing.[323] However, a cascade of events eventually led to PRI's loss of the building in 2012.

In 2007 surging taxes and significant increases in city water and sewer rates severely reduced the building's finances. Due to historic tax credits, property taxes had averaged roughly $6,000 per year, but in 2007, when the tax credits ran out, taxes increased to $85,000 a year. At the same time, water and sewer bills went up by $70,000 a year. Another blow was that expensive building maintenance was needed: the boiler needed to be replaced and the elevators needed maintenance. These financial problems, coupled with decreases in rental income due to some tenants being unable to pay rent during the recession (the "final nail in the coffin," according to Gunter), forced PRI to realize that trying to maintain the building was "a losing battle."[324]

The recession that began in 2008 caused another problem for PRI. In its best years, when construction and renovation were stable, PRI earned a revenue stream with development fees from their clients. When development stopped during the recession, this vital revenue stream dried up.[325]

Consecutive and overlapping events led to PRI's inability to continue paying the Imperial's mortgage. In June 2010, the balance owed on the first mortgage to Fannie Mae was $575,000. PRI determined that they needed $1.1 million to stabilize the building's finances – to pay off the mortgage, make needed repairs, and take care of the most pressing bills.[326]

Ultimately, PRI was unable to work out a solution to solve its fiscal problems. In June 2011, Gunter acknowledged his concern about the situation: "We are out of gas . . . We had a big increase in costs and a decrease in revenues. All of a sudden, we were in a world of hurt." And the Imperial was not the only troubled PRI property. "Literally half our portfolio is under water . . . We are just bone dry," Gunter revealed. PRI estimated that 963 of its 2,100 affordable housing units in Georgia were under financial stress. Unless there was some serious restructuring, PRI feared losing all of the units.[327]

The recession dealt an especially heavy blow because PRI had slim operating margins due to their desire to keep rents as low as possible. There was little room for error. Gunter explained: "Our developments can't withstand that kind of stress because we are marginal at every level . . . The recession just hammered us."[328] Gunter later added, "I remember the helpless feeling when every month the water and sewer bill was higher, and when property taxes made that huge jump. We benefitted from the property tax abatement triggered by our use of historic tax credits, but it turned out that we needed the abatement for a lot longer than the ten-year period. Those costs were quite a large hit to an enterprise that basically broke even."[329]

PRI responded to the recession by reducing staff and restructuring their organization. Additionally, they reduced their properties by 50 percent. The Imperial on Peachtree was one of the properties they let go. In late 2010 it fell into receivership. Gunter was devastated: "As advocates of affordable housing, we would first say: 'Don't lose what you've got, that's going backward . . . That's 20 years of work.'" The properties they kept were left in good shape, but the Imperial, now out of their hands, had an uncertain future. But Gunter acknowledged that there was never a guarantee of a "forever shelf life" for the Imperial and that PRI had provided affordable housing for ten to twelve years at that location. He tried to find something positive in the devastating effects of the economic crisis, a silver lining: "More affordable housing is being created now . . . Rents are down. Housing prices are down. The net effect will be more affordable housing stock that is available through the private market."[330]

The private market, however, did not provide the support services PRI offered at some of its affordable housing units — services that helped transform lives, particularly for people who transitioned from homelessness to housing. "It's a profoundly sad moment," Gunter acknowledged. He indicated that PRI would not give up on affordable housing – they would emerge in a new role, perhaps as an investor in affordable housing and maybe with broader relationships in the community: "We are not stopping. There are no regrets. We are going to move forward."[331] Hopefully, he said, a new owner could continue to provide affordable housing in the building and "we will then celebrate yet another resurrection at the Imperial."[332]

Historian Charles Steffen captures contextual elements of the Imperial's phoenix-like rise under PRI management:

> The Imperial hotel became an Atlanta success story. At a time when the Atlanta Housing Authority was demolishing the city's public housing projects and moving toward a new model of "mixed-income" housing, the Imperial seemed to prove that public-private partnerships offered the best way to shore up the bottom end of the housing market. Backed by a combination of low-income housing tax credits and public subsidies, the city, AHA, and PRI could point to the Imperial as proof that market forces, properly understood and harnessed, held the key to preserving the nation's stock of affordable housing.[333]

But, he concludes, the Imperial's tragic fall revealed the fallacy that all social problems have a market-driven solution. For Steffen, the Imperial Hotel's fate reminds us that "the market is both the creator and destroyer of affordable housing."[334]

Transitions at the Imperial

In January 2012, The Imperial on Peachtree was rescued from foreclosure. An Atlanta-based, for-profit developer of multifamily affordable housing communities (Columbia Residential), and a Columbus, Ohio, non-profit

Above: Interior of an apartment at The Commons at Imperial Hotel, after renovation of The Imperial on Peachtree. Photographer: ©Creative Sources Photography / Rion Rizzo. Photo courtesy of Columbia Residential.

Right: Renovation of The Imperial on Peachtree, 2013. Photo by author.

developer of senior and permanent supportive housing (National Church Residences), purchased the building. In the announcement of their purchase, the new owners indicated that their aim was to "recapitalize" and renovate the building so that it would continue to serve low- to moderate-income residents, including people who were exiting homelessness and others with special needs. They expected to continue offering high quality support services, just as PRI had done.[335]

On March 6, 2014, the new owners held a grand opening and lighting ceremony after the comprehensive renovation was complete. The hotel, renamed The Commons at Imperial Hotel, was opened with 90 units instead of 120. The building systems were replaced, the floor plans were improved, the leasing and management offices were updated, and the space for service providers, amenities, and security was improved. Historic preservation standards remained, even while the building was brought to a sustainable (LEED-certified) energy efficiency standard.[336] Performing the extensive repairs required that the residents relocate during construction.[337]

National Church Services manages the property, including resident services and programming. In their grand opening announcement, they proclaimed:

> The Commons at Imperial Hotel provides permanent supportive housing, or housing with on-site services needed to help the residents stabilize and rebuild their lives through a proven "housing first" model. The renovated building is uniquely designed with the special needs of these residents in mind. Social, educational, therapeutic, vocational and health care services are on-site, including assessment and referral, crisis intervention and integrated behavioral and health care. On-site facilities for residents include a fitness center, health resource room, job training office, laundry room, and library/community room and a resource center – which is equipped with computers and a printer, and community engagement opportunities – such as a woman's group and support groups.[338]

The "housing first" model is a federal approach that strives to place targeted homeless people into permanent housing, provide support services (though residents are not required to participate in them to remain housed), and engage in assertive outreach to homeless people with mental illness who are skeptical of shelters and services. A main goal is to keep people housed. [339]

Like PRI, the new owners used complex, multiple layers of funding to secure the purchase of the building. Discussions between Columbia Residential, National Church Residences, the State of Georgia, and the City of Atlanta were held for a year leading to the purchase of the building. Ultimately, the state provided support for redevelopment and mortgage financing through low income housing tax credits, and the city committed to mortgage financing. Private investment sources also provided much-needed capital for the purchase and renovation of the building.[340]

Chairman and CEO of Columbia Residential, Noel Khalil, whose efforts to create affordable housing included involvement in Welcome House, stated: "We are honored to partner with our city and state to preserve and redevelop the vital housing resource that is now The Commons at Imperial . . . We have made every effort to respect the residents this building will

Exterior of The Commons at Imperial Hotel, after renovation of The Imperial on Peachtree, 2015. Photo by author.

serve and the history of the building in order to reflect the value of our partners' investment and to ensure that the residents have a place they are proud to call their home."[341]

The Imperial Hotel was, once again, resurrected; it would continue to provide shelter and support for Atlanta's low-income residents. The legacy of the hotel occupation would not subside, even after a deep recession nearly shuttered its doors and windows.

Transitions at Welcome House

Like the Imperial Hotel, Welcome House remains open today. In 2000, the Enterprise Foundation awarded PRI's achievement at Welcome House third place in its annual review of affordable housing.[342] In 2009, the composition and rent structure of Welcome House was described as 209 units and one manager's unit, with sizes ranging from 110 to 160 square feet. Additionally, "monthly rents for the tax credit units range from $373 to $425. Units are reserved for tenants from 30% or less of area median income (AMI) on up to 60% or less of AMI. In the Atlanta metro area, 60% of AMI is about $30,000 for an individual and about $43,000 for a four-person household. The average income of Welcome House residents is between $8,000 and $10,000."[343]

In 2009, through federal and state housing tax credits and below-market-rate financing, PRI completed renovation of the property. At a cost of roughly $10 million, they replaced all major systems, added additional common space, mitigated noise, improved wheelchair accessibility, and added energy conservation devices and a rooftop water collection system. Jonathan Toppen, project manager for PRI's developmental services, reported, "About 50% of Welcome House residents have been homeless. Many lived on the streets after institutional care . . . About 50 residents have mental illness, substance abuse, or are wheelchair-bound due to a chronic physical disability. About 20% are veterans."[344]

In 2013, PRI transferred ownership of the building to Project Interconnections, Inc. They, along with their partner, Action Ministries, continue to provide accessible, supportive housing for low-income residents. At the grand reopening, it was announced that the new ownership and management team would continue to offer "the safety net of services to residents [that] can mean a life of independence rather than homelessness, incarceration, or constant institutional care."[345] Bruce Gunter acknowledged that Project Interconnections had for a long time worked with homeless people, and he was certain that Welcome House would continue serving in the spirit of its original purpose.[346]

CHAPTER FIFTEEN
REFLECTIONS ON SUCCESS

The renovation of the Imperial Hotel and the creation of Welcome House are clear and direct legacies of the 1990 hotel occupation. There are other legacies, and generally participants believe that the action was successful, at least in some ways. It is unclear, however, how success should be defined.

John Scruggs considered the occupation a positive event and a "big thing" in Atlanta, even though some of the results were frustrating: "Yes, at that time People for Urban Justice helped these people and me, too. That part was a good thing. But I thought maybe it would progress to where Portman would go in and restore it and put the homeless people in there, but it didn't work that way. That's what I was focusing on. When I heard later that the people that were put out were sleeping on the streets, I just got frustrated with it and moved on." Scruggs said, "If you've got a job and got some money you can stay there, but if you live on the street, you can't. I wouldn't necessarily say it's low income now because they charge good money to stay there."

Robert Dobbins insisted that the occupation was successful, but not without shortcomings, especially regarding what happened at Welcome House shelter, the interim facility that housed some of the hotel occupants: "It was successful, but the money they gave to the people ended up embezzled, and when we opened the shelter up it was supposed to be free, but they started charging fifty cents a day." On a more hopeful note, and in a deeper sense of accomplishment, Dobbins is proud of taking part in the occupation: "We could have gone to jail. It's an event that I'm proud of for the simple reason that we made changes. We made something happen regardless of whether we stuck to it or not. A whole bunch of people together, they can move the world. In the history of Atlanta, the takeover is important."

Dick Rustay described the occupation in terms of bewilderment and accomplishment: "I remember thinking at the time, 'What in heaven's name are we doing?' But we pulled it off!" Dick does not believe there is anything he and Gladys should have done differently during the occupation. "It could have been a year later, and we could have been more experienced," he chuckled. On a more serious note, he added, "But I don't think anyone had the idea that they'd open it up and let people come in. I think that's Eduard's streak of genius that at that spur of the moment he said, 'Just come on in.' It's amazing how things happened. I suspect some of it is that you put yourself in a situation where things can happen. I think that's the key, rather than just staying in your own little world." Dick admitted that his experience with street actions was limited prior to the occupation and that he and others could have been more educated and prepared. But, he reasoned, "If you wait until that happens, then the time passes." He concluded with words of wisdom about prophetic politics: "Not to do it is an action you've taken anyway."

Of all the events that Gladys Rustay has been involved in for over twenty years at the Open Door Community, she believes the hotel occupation was probably the most significant. She remarked, "I think if you get anything these days it's a success because there are such strong currents working against justice and progress." She added, "I think it is important for people to know what is possible if you'll try."

According to Houston Wheeler, the occupation forced city leaders to respond to PUJ's concerns because they learned that threats would be backed up by action. He said, "The true measure of power is to have an impact on the decision-makers. The most powerful impact the occupiers had was to affect the agenda for affordable housing. Developers told me that just the sheer threat of an action or demonstration pushed the city of Atlanta and business community to make decisions and allocate resources for SROs and supportive housing."

The occupation also validated Houston's prophetic ministry in terms of getting out of the church and into the streets: "The whole prophetic dimension of raising our voices and calling for social justice for people who were being abused by the city of Atlanta and the business community set up some parameters for the direction of my ministry. The Open Door and People for Urban Justice validated my sense of a 'call' and the goals were very explicit."

As a symbolic act designed to bring attention to the experiences of Atlanta's homeless people and the structural elements that cause and maintain homelessness, the hotel occupation was a powerful act. Stanley Saunders and Charles Campbell remind us that one aspect of prophetic politics is the act of "street worship," a situation that enables participants to "lay claim to the presence of God in places where the powers of the world evidently reign and continue to crucify Jesus. By naming and giving thanks to God and by proclaiming Jesus as Lord in these spaces, the community seeks to disrupt business as usual."[347]

Dick Rustay explained why the takeover was a vital response to what was happening in Atlanta: "It turned out to be something different than we originally planned. We thought it would just be trespassing and end that way. But it became such a big issue that was in the paper all the time and hundreds of people were involved, which I think was something very special. This brought the homeless situation to the forefront. It was on television every night and in the newspapers. It was simply a watershed." Dick cautioned, however: "I also know there's a tendency to forget and ignore. And I assume that very few people know that the Imperial was an SRO at one time. But it's one of the few victories in that the hotel was refurbished and it has lower income people living there, which is a very powerful thing. Homelessness is something people don't want to talk about now and it's just an accepted reality. It's just built in. And that's a very hard thing. The occupation didn't end anything."

Eduard Loring's writings resonate with Dick's musings: "Today we are a people who accept human beings living on the streets, accept children being eaten by rats under bridges or freezing in abandoned warehouses. We don't care. To our utter shame, we individualists blame the poor for their poverty, just as we believe the rich deserve their plunder."[348] In the meantime, he adds, "children and adults are shoved to the margins of no-justice on the precipice of little-compassion."[349]

Dick is frustrated by what he considers a lack of sustained effort to end homelessness. He believes this stems from a concept in American culture – the idea of housing as an investment to make money instead of housing for shelter. Additionally, he believes people want a quick fix to complex problems:

> It is in the American psyche that we can solve anything in two years and if we can't then we drop it and go on to something else. And this is where I think maybe Pete [Gathje's] point about prophetic politics comes in too, is that you realize homelessness involves a change in how those with homes live. People might be willing to help, but if it impinges upon their lifestyle then there's a tendency to move on. A change of heart and a change of lifestyle – those are very hard things for people to achieve.

One of the lingering results of the occupation is how it forced Dick to contemplate Christian faith:

> We're always talking about public liturgy. Walter Brueggemann talks about how you must acknowledge your pain publicly, that this is the reality of the prophets, all of them did that, especially Jeremiah. This is a part of life that is pretty well lost in our churches, I think. So it's such a foreign, contrary thing, and it's not polite. And this is such a hard thing, especially with middle-class people there is a polite way of doing things, and when you cross over then it is really shocking to people. But sometimes the shock has a point. It goes into people and they have to work with it over a period of time. That is an important part of the Christian faith that is being pretty well lost.

Dick emphasized that in the months leading up to the hotel action people could no longer sit idly by as the city devoted increasing resources to glamorous projects while affordable housing diminished: "That's where this city was moving. The occupation was just trying to say, 'There's no place for homeless people anymore.'"[350]

Sowing Seeds

According to Joe Beasley, the occupation changed a lot of lives in many ways. He believes that it was groundbreaking in that it helped African Americans better understand how to establish affordable housing options for their communities. Prior to the occupation, he commented, "The African American community for the most part didn't know about the not-for-profit sector and how that worked; they didn't know that there were resources available through the government and the state and the city to do some significant things to help poor people. We just didn't know." He said his congregation (Antioch Baptist Church North) was influenced by homelessness and the course of events around the hotel occupation to put together a not-for-profit corporation that began building affordable housing units.

The legacy of the Imperial Hotel occupation is evident in Beasley's work with Antioch Urban Ministries. After collaborating with PRI to develop the Walton House (later re-named the Madison House), Urban Ministries later developed other housing such as Matthew's Place, which provided affordable housing for homeless people with HIV/AIDS. Urban Ministries also worked with Fulton and DeKalb Counties to create housing for people with tuberculosis. "Quite frankly," Joe said, "a lot of things happened from the Imperial. Now we have million-dollar projects on the drawing board and it leads right back to the meeting we had here for the Imperial Hotel." With a sense of accomplishment and pride, he added, "It has worked out quite well":

> It's very hard to quantify these kinds of things, but certainly I saw some new possibilities about how a church can organize itself in a way to get resources so that you could actually begin to tackle some of these problems. And so under the leadership of Rev. Cameron Alexander we put together the Antioch Urban Ministries, a 5013c corporation. We learned that you can save what little money you've got and spend other people's money for good causes, if you structure it right. So we didn't have to put a dime of our money in the Madison, and that was a new revelation to us – all we had to do was follow the rules. When this small corporation was put together I didn't know anything about money and finance, but I was forced to do it because of these events. We were forced to stretch and to expand and necessity was upon us, and when necessity is upon you, then you do what you have to do.

Jo Ann Geary believes that an important aspect of the hotel occupation is that it made homelessness more visible. She said, "I think in a sense we put a face to homelessness. You know, you can talk about homelessness and hear it on the news, but until you really put a face on it, it's kind of out there somewhere. I don't think we made any big strides in terms of the housing issue, but I feel quite confident that we did change some people's hearts. I think that's where it starts."

In particular, Jo Ann thinks that PUJ offered a model for other Christians to follow, especially when church groups delivered supplies to the hotel: "They saw us interacting with homeless men, women, and children, and when they came, then I think they were interacting in a different way than they may have before. Once you put a face on something it changes your view." Jo Ann is describing one of the goals of the Open Door: reducing the distance between housed and un-housed people. When that distance is reduced, ignorance and fear can dissolve.

Jo Ann reflected upon the foundations of Christianity: "When you say radical I think of going to the root, and I think the root or the foundation, the very underpinnings of our faith are love and charity, and if we don't have that for one another and show compassion and care, we've missed the message of Christ." She continued, "And so really the only way Jesus comes into our world again and again is through us in what we do and how we do it. If Jesus is going to live, it's because of people, not because of institutions or buildings."

Geary enthusiastically agrees with Peter Maurin's notion that there is "dynamite" in the gospel: "I think of the gospel as Jesus' life and when I think of how he lived his life, that is dynamic, that is dynamite, that is radical, that is revolutionary. And we just need to continue to be courageous, willing to not only believe that, but to put that into practice, to put it into action."[351]

CHAPTER SIXTEEN
OPEN DOOR ACTIVISM

The hotel takeover enacted prophetic politics when Open Door residents and the radical remnant took to the streets to proclaim the sense of injustice they perceived in the dearth of affordable housing. This "impolite" method of protest conflicted with Atlanta's governing regime. Houston Wheeler contextualized the Imperial Hotel occupation:

> The civil rights movement, in terms of protest, did not have a very visible face in Atlanta. This is Martin Luther King Jr.'s hometown, but I think the city of Atlanta and the business community have a real problem with conflict. The governing regime doesn't show their dirty laundry in public and that's what PUJ did. As I say in *The Other Atlanta* one of the more effective methods of community organizing is embarrassment, and that's what the Imperial Hotel takeover did. The Atlanta business community does not do very well with handling embarrassment. I think it's their Achilles heel. The city of Atlanta and the business community try to shame those who use that methodology as if to say, "That's not the way we do things here in Atlanta."

Wheeler continued, "Protesting is the heart of our democracy. It's the heart of prophetic ministry and our civil rights history. The civil rights movement is applauded here, but they suggest 'you can do protesting outside of Atlanta but not here, because we handle things differently, we handle things behind closed doors.'" Representative John Lewis, a longtime political leader in Georgia and a major figure in the civil rights movement, points to why Atlanta's leaders eschew public protest. He remarked, "The city of Atlanta is very image-conscious. There [is] a great [deal] of pride, but we want to protect our community. We don't want any blemishes to come out into the public and the business community is probably more sensitive than any other segment."[352]

Drawing from decades of experience engaging some of the "powers and principalities" that create and sustain homelessness and poverty, Eduard Loring encourages people to consider the consequences of conforming to "acceptable" behavior:

> We have learned through suffering and death. Many of us white folks of good will now know through our loss of soul that: Silence = Betrayal, Silence = Violence, Silence = Death. Domination works in the midst of our manners and fears. We are afraid of conflict and confrontation. We are afraid of rejection and job loss if we speak the truth in love to power and peers. We are taught not to raise our voices, not to contradict our hosts or those in authority. And in our silence and politeness, children die. We die. Violence is accepted . . . We are polite, respectable and complicit in the blood and anguish of the victims of our manners. No nail driven by the hammers of the powers of oppression and domination has pierced the incarnation of God's Word like manners and respectability, those demons who nest and infest our lives by bringing comfort.[353]

Eduard's words are a clarion call for bold, bodily, direct action; for those who understand the message and heed the call, they show a route from darkness to light. People for Urban Justice and the Open Door Community refused to remain idle in the midst of poor people's suffering, so they raised their voices and engaged their bodies in street preaching. The outcome of these actions was uncertain, so enormous courage was summoned to participate.

Elizabeth Dede, one of the "Imperial Eight," shared her ideas about stepping in when there is conflict:

> I have this peculiar notion about courage and it requires a little bit of foolishness, sort of the idea of being a fool for Christ. You go into these things having no clear idea about what is going to happen, but you know at the outset that much is going to be

required of you and that you are ill-prepared. You know you won't have any idea of how to respond to it, and that often you will respond inappropriately. In the end you'll have regrets, and you'll wish that you had responded differently. But also in the end I have found that you are most often pretty amazed at how the Holy Spirit works and the astounding outcome. I think we've been tremendously blessed in our actions.

Jo Ann Geary remarked:

We need the contemplative, but also someone that's willing to stand up and walk the walk as well as talk the talk. Taking an issue that is close to your heart and trying to make a difference, to stand up and know that anytime you look at an injustice and bring it to the forefront you are seen as the troublemaker, then you are setting up a real conflict. And those are not comfortable situations. But being willing to put yourself in an uncomfortable situation to bring forth something you think needs to be brought forth, something that needs to be done, and to show some urgency around an issue, well that isn't a comfortable thing to do, because you know you are going to get flack, and people are going to resent you, and people are going to misunderstand you. But you've got to come out of yourself. You've got to look at the issue and do what you can rather than being worried about what people might say about you or what people might think about you.

Murphy Davis viewed the occupation in a larger context:

The Imperial Hotel occupation is a supreme example for me because what we planned didn't happen at all. We made all these plans but then what happened was a completely different thing. And we could never in a million years have planned what happened. It was that sense of, okay, we *have* to do something. And so we're going take a risk and plan this action. And then it didn't work at all. We felt like it had totally failed. It's like what Dorothy Day says: "All we have is a few loaves and a couple of fish, so we offer them and God does the rest." And it's like the piddly little plans we made. We offered those as a gift and God took them and made them into something we could have never imagined. How could you ever imagine planning those sixteen days where there were no major disasters? Nobody got hurt. There was a level of community and solidarity built that was absolutely astounding. And it was that way until Shirley Franklin spent the night in the hotel and began to undermine the entire action. She worked, she lied, she manipulated, and she betrayed. Until that happened, there was such strength and unity. You just can't go out and organize that.

Murphy's comment about People for Urban Justice's "piddly little plans" and Dede's ideas about courage resonate with Stanley Saunders and Charles Campbell's words:

Whether through direct speech or through other, more creative approaches, preachers confronting the powers will find ways to expose them. At times such resistance will indeed seem fragile, puny, and foolish. At other times, the preacher will meet with opposition or create conflict. At all times, such preaching will require imagination and courage. Nevertheless, the vocation of the preacher as a "keeper of the Word" is to speak the truth and expose the powers. In the midst of babel, such truthtelling is essential for the life of the church and the redemption of the world.[354]

In terms of social justice work, Gladys Rustay did not believe that the Open Door would crush or even crack the powers they were up against; rather, she said they will continue to "chip away" at them. Even after a tough defeat, she said, the Open Door does not give up. For Gladys, there are two central components of the Open Door Community: works of mercy and social justice work. Balancing both is difficult. She seeks solace by determining where her efforts are most effective. For now, Gladys says she and Dick will do, in former Open Door Community resident Willie Dee Wimberly's words, "the best we can until we can't."

Confronting a Powerful Regime

Open Door Community residents and the radical remnant chip away at Atlanta's power structure. It is a difficult battle. While Atlanta's mayors have held significant power, there is no denying that Central Atlanta Progress, the Chamber of Commerce, and the Action Forum, when considered in tandem, hold great power.

According to Clarence Stone, Central Atlanta Progress (CAP) has been the central element of the governing coalition, the regime.[355] "In Atlanta," Stone asserts, "the impression develops quickly that all civic roads lead to CAP. It is hard to make a broad-based civic effort without tying into CAP's network."[356] Action Forum, for example, an organization that linked white business leaders and top-level African American leaders, was created by CAP in 1969. Stone explains how Action Forum worked and what was accomplished along racial lines for the governing regime: "All of the white participants were chief executive officers of major businesses. Black participants came from more diverse backgrounds – social and volunteer-agency heads and college presidents as well as business executives. They met informally and quietly once a month, with no officers or minutes, for frank and open discussion about major community issues."[357] These meetings facilitated the inclusion of African Americans in the economic life of the white business elite and, subsequently, not only were African Americans named to the boards of major white businesses, but, eventually, some landed executive positions with major corporations such as Coca-Cola and Delta Airlines.[358]

Through CAP, Action Forum, and the Chamber of Commerce, middle-class African Americans gained access to economic power while, simultaneously, elite whites gained access to city hall, an increasingly important task considering the racial shift from minority black to majority black in the 1970s. Stone's astute observations illuminate central elements of the governing regime: "It would be an overstatement to suggest that the white business elite has created a black leadership in its own image, but it is no exaggeration that the network of civic cooperation pulls black leadership strongly in that direction."[359] Further, Stone contends, "The system of interaction was not one concerned with race relations in general; rather, it was a set of planned racial arrangements that linked elements of the black middle class closely with white business interests."[360] In sum, each of the entities got what it wanted, but it was not racial harmony based on altruism, but rather self-interest.[361]

Stanley Saunders and Charles Campbell characterize the power structure in Atlanta:

African Americans make up the majority in the city and have held the position of mayor since 1973. However, this African American majority and the succession of African American mayors have learned that the path toward substantive change runs through the white-dominated coalition of downtown business leaders, Central Atlanta Progress, which greatly limits the power of the city government. In addition, because much of metro Atlanta's wealth lies outside the "city limits," the economic needs of the city proper are often held hostage to the wishes of residents of the outlying suburbs. While African Americans may hold the political offices, white Atlantans usually hold the economic strings. City officials consequently often lack not only the power, but also the resources to address the city's problems.[362]

Eduard Loring asks, "Have they damned democracy?" He describes Atlanta's situation even more starkly:

Dr. King, Black prophet, oft said, "Life's most persistent and urgent question is, what are you doing for others?" But rapacious Central Atlanta Progress and the avaricious Atlanta City Council's "most persistent and urgent question" is "how much money did you make today? What did you do today to rid our city of the poor Black and homeless ones?" Love might be an answer, but jail is the only solution, says the power elite of Atlanta's White Male Supremacy system.[363]

Street Advocacy across Race and Class Lines

An important aspect of the hotel occupation was the way that people of different races, classes, and genders built alliances for social change. Houston Wheeler believed that People for Urban Justice (and by extension the Open Door Community) provided important leadership for social justice movements in Atlanta in the 1990s:

Historically, the Southern Christian Leadership Conference was the civil rights organization that was involved in protests, actions, and events throughout the Southeast. But there was not a whole lot of it in Atlanta. In Atlanta, PUJ was the civil rights leader in the 90s. We were the organization that was pushing things that were on the cutting edge, and I think everybody sensed that. When we had PUJ planning meetings for additional actions it energized us spiritually and organizationally. We were hungry: we were ready to keep pressing and to keep the pressure on. We felt like the Imperial Hotel action was such a success in terms of how we felt spiritually that God was working through us to be an advocate, to communicate to the entire community, especially the business community and the city of Atlanta, that poor and homeless people had a voice through PUJ."

Robert Dobbins, a homeless African American man, stayed in the Imperial for seven days during the occupation. Robert worked to bring attention to the political reasons for the shortage of affordable housing in Atlanta. Reflecting on the occupation, Robert acknowledged the importance of alliances across race and class boundaries: "We had someone backin' us up. If a homeless man starts something for a good cause, and he ain't got somebody for a foundation to back him up, they're gonna separate everybody. But if you got somebody backing you up like a church or a community, something like the Open Door, or anybody that is going to be a spokesperson for you, and they ain't homeless but they're still helping with the cause, well that's what I'm talking about."

Dobbins's sense of having someone "back him up" is based on cultural truths evident in the United States. Stanley Saunders and Charles Campbell explain: "In this culture, ownership of land, houses, cars, and other possessions is a primary means for the expression of identity. With property comes power; ownership makes one a person to be reckoned with. When we lose the resources to purchase property, we also lose voice, political presence, and the capacity to construct 'personal space' and define our own identity. Those who have power express it not only in the private realm, however, but publicly."[364]

While acknowledging that PUJ was adamant that white, middle-class people not control the occupation and negotiations, Jo Ann Geary wondered if they should have taken more control of negotiations: "I felt sad that when all was said and done, when they met with Franklin and someone involved with Portman to negotiate going to a different place, a shelter, I [wished] we could have had the time to mentor them more." Echoing Murphy Davis's comments, she added, "I think that when you are trying to negotiate from a place of nothingness, when you have nothing, and you are dealing with these powerful people, you'll almost take anything, and that saddened me, because I felt like there wasn't a level playing field," Jo Ann explained:

> They were told "yes we're going to try to do this" and "we're going to take you to Welcome House" and it was a lot of verbiage and it sounded good and they grabbed at it. They took it, whereas I think if we were more involved in the negotiations we'd say, "What exactly are you saying? What exactly does this mean? You are saying you'll do something about housing, well what is your strategy? What is your plan? Is there a timeline?" And of course they wouldn't ask those questions.

Ultimately, Geary believes that the Executive Committee's inexperience in negotiating led to the final outcome. She added that they did the best they could given their inexperience and the conditions under which they negotiated. She called the final result a "real eye opener" and an "unfortunate situation." She suggested that if PUJ members were less sensitive to race, class, and power issues they may have inserted themselves more forcefully into negotiations; however, in no way did PUJ want to be the "powerful white folks" wresting control of negotiations. She exclaimed, "It wasn't our place to do that. That would not have been right. The only other thing we could have done is impose ourselves, and none of us wanted to do that. That would not have been right either."

Joe Beasley insisted that bridging communities was an essential component of PUJ. He suggested that African Americans are sometimes suspicious of white people's motives: "There's still a group of people who think that when white people come out to help the poor that there's some kind of ulterior motive." Other people, he said, disparage those who make homelessness their vocation: "There are other people saying that homelessness is a vocation for some of these white bleeding hearts, and it's where they get their money from and they've got a vested interest in keeping us homeless." Beasley views these reactions as cynical: "I don't buy into it and I think people that see it that way don't really have the big picture." But he admitted that he is no expert: "I'm not suggesting that I have the big picture totally, but one thing that African Americans have to be clear on is that we've always had the abolitionists. They were here from day one and they weren't a huge group, but they were dying for the struggle for justice and they are still here – this group is still here, like Murphy and Eduard, for example."

Passion filled Beasley's voice when he contemplated Murphy Davis and Eduard Loring's works of hospitality: "That whole stretch of Ponce de Leon would be different if the Open Door wasn't there. Eduard is a white man who is intelligent, and that has its privileges, but he is not going to tolerate the police coming in and dragging people out of his house."[365] Joe read about a complaint from a neighbor who lives near the Open Door. The neighbor complained about the large number of people milling around the Open Door and in the neighborhood. The neighbor viewed the situation with anger, but Joe saw it differently: "The Open Door's backyard is full of people; I think it's the most spiritual spot in town."

Eduard describes the Open Door geography in broad historical terms: "Place: The Open Door Community front yard. Former Creek Nation Land. Former territory of the Confederate States of America. Today, sanctuary for the disinherited."[366] He acknowledges the ways that neighbors view the Open Door Community: "For some of our neighbors, we are the cause of homelessness and hunger in Atlanta. To others, volunteers and supporters, we are a point of light in the dark night of White Male Supremacist housing patterns and food distribution. We carry on, do what we can do, and wait for the crumbling of the USA's Berlin Wall."[367] He adds, "Our yard is a sanctuary from police, Confederate flags, neo-Nazis, white teenagers hurting the homeless for humor, and white business elites who see the future of downtown Atlanta as free from abandoned people, particularly Black men . . . We are chinking the wall of domination. To some of our guests, the Open Door front yard is a holy place of shared life and love."[368]

Beasley understood that advocacy is risky. "If you want to stand up for justice," he warned, "you can't be fainthearted, and you can't be made to feel you're not civil. If you stand up for justice, you're gonna have to be willing to really step on some toes, to stomp on some toes, and the louder they scream you have to scream back for justice, that's what Ed and Murphy do." Joe's comments illustrate the idea that alliances for social justice across race, class, and gender categories exist. He said that working with Murphy and Eduard over the years has been a tremendous living example of what it means to struggle for justice when you do not have to: "They could cruise for the rest of their lives if they wanted to, and instead of sharing the big old house on Ponce they could just do it like everybody else and say 'get your black ass out of here,' but they don't."

Jo Ann Geary, a seasoned Sister and nurse who had spent time with Dorothy Day in New York's Bowery, fondly recalled how she became involved in the Open Door Community: "They were one of the houses of hospitality and they just did it so beautifully. I was in many shelters where I'd go in the evenings and set up a clinic, or during soup kitchen time in church halls, and God bless them for that, but the Open Door did it in such a gracious way. People were seated. They were spoken to. They were treated compassionately. It was a whole different environment – no assembly line mentality." For Jo Ann, the Open Door treats people with dignity and respect regardless of race, faith, or position in society. She recalled, "I realized that they had a Eucharist on Sundays and I started going to that, and I felt at home, a kindred spirit to so many of the people." In addition to attending Sunday Eucharist, she set up a weekly clinic at the Open Door where she administered medication and treatment to homeless people.

Jo Ann believes that it is imperative that people continue to be called to account if their actions (or inaction) warrant it. "That's what we need to be about," she urged. "To do justice, to love kindly," is important, she said. "But," she continued, "it takes courage, it takes persistence, it takes faith, it takes love. It takes community. It's hard to do alone. And that's what I think was so beautiful with the Open Door. We didn't always have to agree on different issues or how to go about things or whatever, but our basic understanding, our thrust is always the same: to love one another, to do justice, to give voice to the voiceless."

CHAPTER SEVENTEEN
KEEP ON KEEPING ON AT THE OPEN DOOR

Despite a range of potential difficulties, People for Urban Justice and homeless people fashioned alliances inside the Imperial Hotel. In *Poor People's Movements*, Frances Fox Piven and Richard Cloward indicate, "For a protest movement to arise out of these traumas of daily life, people have to perceive the deprivation and disorganization they experience as both wrong, and subject to redress. The social arrangements that are ordinarily perceived as just and immutable must come to seem both unjust and mutable."[369] They explain this process:

> The emergence of a protest movement entails a transformation both of consciousness and of behavior. The change in consciousness has at least three distinct aspects. First, "the system" – or those aspects of the system that people experience and perceive – loses legitimacy. Large numbers of men and women who ordinarily accept the authority of their rulers and the legitimacy of institutional arrangements come to believe in some measure that these rulers and those arrangements are unjust and wrong. Second, people who are ordinarily fatalistic, who believe that existing arrangements are inevitable, begin to assert "rights" that imply demands for change. Third, there is a new sense of efficacy; people who ordinarily consider themselves helpless come to believe that they have some capacity to alter their lot.[370]

Piven reminds us that in the classical view of social movement theory, "hardship itself propels people to collective defiance, especially in the context of growing concentrations of income and wealth." [371] But, she explains, "people endure hardship more often than they protest it, and even extreme inequality does not necessarily lead people to see their circumstances as unjust."[372] And this is particularly true when cultural and political strategies construct these circumstances as inevitable. [373]

Theologian Walter Brueggemann points out what PUJ and homeless people were up against in their opposition to the "powers and principalities" of the established governing regime and the status quo that it traditionally builds: "The church, in its contestation, must always work in such a way, because the dominant and defining categories of reality, mistaken as they are, occupy a lot of space and administer a lot of hardware. In the face of such formidable force, the claims of this public theology are not easy or obvious or readily persuasive. These claims must always be made from the underside, in a way that seeks to enter the unguarded pores of dominant assumptions."[374]

Similarly, Piven and Cloward write, "Common sense and historical experience combine to suggest a simple but compelling view of the roots of power in any society. Crudely but clearly stated, those who control the means of physical coercion, and those who control the means of producing wealth, have power over those who do not."[375]

Of course, ideologically, those in power also control what is considered wrong and right – what is considered acceptable behavior and what is not. Homeless people feel the pressures from above far more powerfully than those of other classes. Piven and Cloward explain: "Those for whom the rewards are most meager, who are the most oppressed by inequality, are also acquiescent. Sometimes they are the most acquiescent, for they have little defense against the penalties that can be imposed for defiance."[376]

Maynard Jackson and Shirley Franklin were savvy about how to use power to their advantage against those who defied them. Both were well versed in the stratagems of power. Following at least one strand of social movement theory, Jackson's and Franklin's efforts to work *with* homeless people were first and foremost a strategy to quell the force of insurgency that confronted them.[377] To put it bluntly, they needed to get the occupants out of the hotel. Jackson and Franklin likely knew that insurgency is always short-lived and that "once it subsides and people leave the streets, most of the organizations which it temporarily threw up and which elites helped to nurture simply fade away."[378] This is what was so effective about Franklin's plan to lure occupants out of the hotel with temporary shelter and the promise of jobs.

The Welcome House temporary shelter, as a form of homeless self-empowerment, was doomed from the start. Piven and Cloward explain why:

> Ordinarily, of course, elites do not support efforts to form organizations of lower-class people. But when insurgency wells up, apparently uncontrollable, elites respond. And one of their responses is to cultivate those lower-class organizations which begin to emerge in such periods, for they have little to fear from organizations, especially from organizations which come to depend upon them for support. Thus, however unwittingly, leaders and organizers of the lower classes act in the end to facilitate the efforts of elites to channel the insurgent masses into normal politics, believing all the while that they are taking the long and arduous but certain path to power. When the tumult is over, these organizations usually fade, no longer useful to those who provided the resources necessary to their survival. Or the organization persists by becoming increasingly subservient to those on whom it depends.[379]

Put simply, those in power would never allow those who oppose them to have the resources to have a sustained oppositional force – it defies logic. Rather, the powerful subvert and subsume oppositional forces by whatever means necessary. The shelter was merely a means to treat a symptom instead of a malady.

Eduard Loring suggests that, overall, "we accomplish so little, hardly a mustard seed at all. Not enough; hardly anything."[380] And yet, if we consider what *was* accomplished under the particular circumstances presented, the Imperial Hotel occupation can be seen as having at least limited success. Put another way, "The relevant question to ask is whether, on balance, the movement made gains or lost ground; whether it advanced the interests of [poor] people or set back those interests."[381] Clearly, the interests of poor people were advanced, at least minimally: affordable housing *was* developed. Moreover, activists and organizations individually and collectively built upon the occupation's foundation. Instead of measuring the occupation based on what was *not* accomplished (3,500 units of affordable housing, the elimination of homelessness), it is perhaps more appropriate to consider what *was possible* under the conditions present during and after the occupation.[382]

We must not forget the intangible power unleashed when People for Urban Justice opened the hotel door and encouraged people from the streets to join them. When that door was opened a literal and figurative joining of hands occurred. Through this bond, housed and un-housed people acted in concert with their guts and their hearts. They were defiant, they challenged traditional authorities, they transgressed rules and laws laid down by authorities, they demanded redress for their grievances.[383] Piven and Cloward astutely inform us: "A placid poor get nothing, but a turbulent poor sometimes get something."[384]

American history has witnessed many such events, "from the first uprisings by freeholders, tenants, and slaves in colonial America, to the postrevolutionary debtor rebellions, through the periodic eruptions of strikes and riots by industrial workers, to the ghetto riots of the twentieth century."[385] There is tremendous power in these insurgencies because "in each instance, masses of the poor were somehow able, if only briefly, to overcome the shame bred by a culture which blames them for their plight."[386] It is essential to keep in mind that "when protest does arise, when masses of those who are ordinarily docile become defiant, a major transformation has occurred . . . *Only under exceptional conditions are the lower classes afforded the socially determined opportunity to press for their own class interests.*"[387]

A message must be clear: on June 18, 1990, when PUJ opened the hotel door and homeless people – the outcasts, the despised, the feared – began occupying it, success transpired as candles illuminated darkness on the first night of sixteen nights in the Imperial Hotel.

Jo Ann Geary captured central tenets of PUJ and the Open Door Community when she remarked:

> God is love. If I can't reach and do for the person in front of me and love that person, how can I love something that I can't see? I think your beliefs, your faith is something given to you and it's so deep that it can't be denied. I think we all express it differently, but you are my Brother, and she is my Sister. We've got to reach out to each other and help each other. And when we see something

that isn't right, we have to speak up, we've got to be that voice for the voiceless. When people are very poor and powerless, they don't have a voice; who is listening to them if they speak out? So I think you become that voice. When you think of Jesus' life, he went against a lot – the church of that day, the heresies, and the heretics. He was a revolutionary. He wasn't about the law; he was about the spirit. Yes, you've got to have laws of society to govern the whole, but if that's all you have and you have no spirit, and you can't see the individual person there, hurting . . . you've missed it; you don't have love in your heart.

Despite pessimism about what People for Urban Justice accomplished through the occupation, Eduard suggests that "Out of our anguished radical politics and hopeful faith springs forth the love and compassion to keep on keeping on" at the Open Door and on Atlanta's streets.[388] He calls us to action: "This is the gift of life: the gift of hunger and thirst for righteousness and justice. We are companions on a journey, a life of reducing the distance and moving into solidarity with the disinherited who live East of Eden. Yea, all of us live East of Eden (John Steinbeck). Here the dove and the hawk are in a battle to the end. Which side are you on? Oh, which side are you on?"[389]

There are more voices to raise and more chains to break in the ongoing effort to build the Beloved Community. Prophetic politics requires sincerity, sacrifice, courage, and determination. Prophetic politics demands brash bodies. PUJ activists, led by the initial "Imperial Eight," courageously put their bodies on the line for affordable housing in Atlanta.

EPILOGUE

Within a week after the Imperial Hotel occupation ended, *Atlanta Journal-Constitution* associate editor Cynthia Tucker – African American, Left leaning, and influential – claimed that "militancy" was passé in Atlanta. Writing about the occupation with a disdainful tone, Tucker asserted that Atlanta's "upwardly mobile black professionals" found street antics such as those by Rev. Hosea Williams (and by extension People for Urban Justice) "amusing when they are not aggravating."[390] Further, she claimed that "idealists" such as Eduard Loring, whose suspicion of big business was "left over from the 1960s," were merely "tilt[ing] at windwills."

According to Tucker, Loring and PUJ simplified the complexity of the situation and created an imaginary foe when they took to the streets urging city leaders to pay attention to affordable housing. Tucker, apparently accepting the imaginary virtues of "trickle down" economics, a theory with wide appeal in the 1980s and pushed by a smoke-and-mirrors Hollywood actor, President Ronald Reagan, suggested that urban revitalization and a stronger tax base (hence, middle- and upper-class prosperity) was a vital engine for affordable housing development. Tucker was not *necessarily* wrong about this, but she was unimaginative, seemingly so caught up in the wonders and wizardry of gentrification and urban revitalization that she could not envision another way to address affordable housing development. Rather than offer creative alternatives of her own, she instead belittled Loring, who, she said, "harks back to a time when answers were easy, federal money flowed freely and sit-ins brought change. That was a while back."

Tucker was wrong about protests. Street actions were not passé in 1990. Loring and PUJ were not dusty relics. Civil disobedience in the post-civil rights era continued to reap rewards. In fact, a legacy of the "militant" Imperial Hotel occupation included a wave of affordable housing that was developed in ensuing years. Andrew Mickle, the judge who presided over the six PUJ activists' courtroom appearance following the occupation, asserted that a lot happened to accommodate homeless people in the years following the occupation, and he suggested that perhaps the takeover was where it got its "jumpstart." Of course, those accommodations were collaborative efforts uniting the vision, knowledge, skills, and energy of a wide range of people, from activists to developers to politicians and others.

Craig Taylor, a long-time developer whose knowledge of affordable housing development in Atlanta is both vast and deep, called the occupation "a lightning strike." For Taylor, the takeover energized the development of affordable housing during the 1990s:

> All of this was made possible starting with Eduard Loring and advocacy and hard-hitting prophecy about the evil, if you will, of systematic bias generated in the city. It's not that there were people who were saying "these homeless don't deserve this," it's that the systems were set up in such a way that they weren't going to serve that population. And by agitating, Eduard Loring and company were able to call that out in a prophetic way in the true sense of spiritual prophecy, and prick consciences all over the place and generate the momentum that led to the success of [affordable housing development].

The Imperial Hotel renovation and the creation of Welcome House are direct legacies of the occupation, but other affordable housing units are rooted in the occupation, at least by some measure, if we consider that the occupation influenced political will and tapped financial streams. These units include Walton House, Edgewood Center, Bethlehem Inn, Santa Fe Villas, O'Hearn House, Hope House, and others. Indirect influence is difficult to measure, but it seems likely that the occupation also spurred the creation or resurgence of homeless advocacy groups.

After the occupation, Taylor witnessed "the dominoes starting to fall." But as Taylor, Bruce Gunter, and others know, affordable housing cannot be accomplished alone. To harness activists' energy and to build housing, collaboration between bankers, politicians, developers, and others is vital.

Taylor and Gunter acknowledge that there were many people who influenced political will or channeled funding during the wave of housing development after the occupation. The list includes Atlanta Housing Commissioners Scott Carlson, Carl Hartrampf, and Paul Stange; State Housing Trust Fund Commission chair Bill Bolling; Senator Wyche Fowler; and executive director of the Georgia Supportive Housing Association, Paul Bolster. Murphy Davis added that Susan May, executive director of Project Interconnections (1990-1996), an organization that develops permanent housing with on-site support for homeless and mentally ill adults, was a vital figure in affordable housing development. Of course, there are many others who labored in ways large and small to create affordable housing during the post-occupation years.

Sometimes timing is a key component in affordable housing development. For example, Taylor observed that after the economic turmoil caused by the savings and loan crisis of the late 1980s, massive property foreclosures – nationwide and in Atlanta – opened up the possibility of purchasing buildings at below-market-rate prices. In fact, PRI purchased the Walton at a reasonable price because it was in foreclosure. An "unsung hero" in Atlanta's wave of affordable housing development, Taylor proclaimed, is Ernie Eden, who worked for Freddie Mac (the Federal Home Loan Mortgage Corporation); he funneled foreclosed housing stock to non-profit groups, who then renovated the units for affordable housing.

Taylor understands the scope of collaboration that is necessary for affordable housing development. He said, "You take the in-your-face, non-equivocating advocates [activists]; you take the do-gooders who are trying to reform and make something happen [housing developers]; but without the third piece – the politicians and bureaucrats, the ones who control the system – without their vision, leadership, and courage, you're not going to get much change." Of course, vision, leadership, and courage are required from all involved. For Taylor, the lightning strike that energized the wave of affordable housing development in the 1990s was a "beautiful time in Atlanta when all of this came together, and for a space of about five years we really changed this, we really made a difference." He added, "That perfect storm has not happened again."[391]

The long-term legacy of the occupation included affordable housing; the short-term legacy included a series of surprises that demonstrated that prophetic politics, or "foot theology" (walking the walk as well as talking the talk), can be a vital tool in civic engagement and civil discourse that can build foundations for long-term goals. In handwritten notes, Murphy Davis captured the "Imperial Surprises":

1. More than [we] prayed for – six hours to sixteen days
2. Action on behalf of homeless people
3. The most powerful action by homeless people in Atlanta's history
4. Attracting the attention of city officials to housing the homeless
5. Completely tying up the mayor's staff for three days, including the mayor himself for more than half a day and evening[392]

About that battle on Peachtree Street and beyond . . . Who won? The building of the Beloved Community, though sometimes fraught with tension and anger, is not a battle – it is a spiritual, emotional, and intellectual process. Core ingredients for the Community include faith, trust, and empathy. The foundation is laid. The mortar is ready. It is time for activists, developers, politicians, business leaders, and others to grab a hammer; to revive the courage, commitment, and collaboration that characterized Atlanta in the mid-1990s; and to energize, organize, and prioritize affordable housing development. Three thousand five hundred units of SRO housing have not been developed . . . *yet*. People still live on the streets . . . *but* people still care.

I hope that in this book you have discovered people you can admire for their commitment to affordable housing, no matter how they plied their trade – activist, developer, politician, or banker. When considering the vagaries of affordable housing development, Houston Wheeler perceptively observed, "everybody has his or her role." Workers young and old, Left and Right, Christian and non-Christian, activist and politician, developer and neighbor . . . It is time to build a building.

> Yes, a miracle did indeed happen at the Imperial Hotel. But it was not a miracle stumbled upon by fate or by chance; no, this miracle arose out of sweat and persistence, out of a few folks' gritty determination to see a dream realized. May we all find the courage to sweat our way toward more such miracles.[393]
> — Stacia Brown, *Hospitality*, 1997

Final + Signed Draft.

STATE OF GEORGIA

COUNTY OF FULTON

Signed July 18, 1990

Same day we went To court!

MEMORANDUM OF UNDERSTANDING

WHEREAS, there are an estimated 10,000 homeless persons in the City of Atlanta; and

WHEREAS, Single Room Occupancy facilities (SRO) can provide better housing with more dignity than shelters at a cost within the ability to pay of the homeless who are better able to get employment when living in an SRO setting; and

WHEREAS, SROs have been demolished throughout Atlanta in recent years, and new production of SROs depends upon regulatory and financial assistance from the City; and

WHEREAS, the Mayor of the City of Atlanta and the Executive Committee of Welcome House, composed of homeless people, have agreed to work together to help solve the problems of homelessness; and

WHEREAS, the Mayor is committed to the effort to identify, coordinate, support and implement programs to meet the needs of the City's homeless population. This commitment recognizes the importance of increased participation from all sectors of the Metropolitan Atlanta community: public, private and religious.

NOW, THEREFORE, the Mayor of the City of Atlanta and the Executive Committee of Welcome House declare the following:

1.   The Mayor commits his administration to produce a net increase of 3,500 units of SRO housing over the next 3 1/2 years. This will include production of 1,000 units per year, with the first units started no later than September 1, 1990. No single project shall exceed 200 units.

2.   The target rental rate shall be $49 per week/$7 per day. At least 1,000 of the 3,500 units shall be available at that price and priority for City approval and assistance shall be given to proposals which maximize the number of units at that rental rate. All parties shall exercise their best efforts to achieve the lowest rental rate.

3.   The Mayor, or his designee, shall consult regularly with
an SRO Advisory Committee on site selection, project design,
selection of developers/contractors, hiring of minorities/
homeless people, structure of ownership of approved projects and
overall direction of the SRO program. The Committee, in
consultation with the staff of the City, shall develop a list of
existing facilities to be designated the "SRO existing facility"
list, which shall be presented to the City Council.

The Committee shall consist of 17 persons, 9 to be selected by
the Executive Committee of Welcome House, the remainder to be
appointed by the Mayor. The Mayor's appointees shall include
other citizens, the Taskforce on the Homeless and the
Metropolitan Christian Council.

4.   The Mayor shall propose legislation to the City Council
amending the zoning ordinance of the City to allow SROs as a
permitted use, not requiring a conditional permit, in all commercial, industrial and high density residential zones (16+ per
acre). The Mayor shall also propose legislation discouraging the
demolition of existing SROs as well as buildings with potential
for use as SROs, including the requirement, upon demolition of
any unit appearing on the "SRO existing facility list", of a 1
for 1 replacement of that unit. (For purposes of calculating the
3,500 unit commitment, these replacement units would not be
counted because they would not represent a net increase in
available facilities.)

5.   Up to 185 homeless persons shall be accomodated, free of
charge, at a facility at Memorial Drive, to be named "Welcome
House." The ultimate direction of the facility shall be under
Jerome Eppinger, or a person designated by the City to replace
him, but the day-to-day management shall be provided by the
Welcome House Executive Committee. Such management shall be
consistent with applicable local, state and federal regulations
regarding such facilities. This facility would be open to women
and children as well as men, the facility may stay open 24 hours
a day and the Executive Committee may allocate spaces on other
than a daily "first come first served" basis.

Recognizing the desire to differentiate this facility from
most shelters, the Mayor shall provide the services of an
architect to consult with the Executive Committee concerning
possible physical modifications of the facility and shall make

2

available resources to effectuate a reasonable amount of modifications.

This, the 3rd day of July, 1990.

_____
Mayor, City of Atlanta

EXECUTIVE COMMITTEE, WELCOME HOUSE

BY:_____
     BILL JONES, Chairperson

_____
WILLIAM TOLBERT, Secretary/Treasurer

_____
BOBBY D. MUHAMMAD, Co-Vice Chairperson

_____
MICHAEL ALLEN, Co-Vice Chairperson

3

"Imperial Eight" Biographies

Below are brief 1990 biographies of the eight people who broke into the Imperial Hotel, and the statements that they made prior to the break-in. At the end of each entry is an update highlighting events in their lives since the occupation.

Murphy Davis, 42, is an ordained Presbyterian minister, founding partner of the Open Door Community, and director of Southern Prison Ministry in Georgia.

Murphy's statement for the Imperial Hotel street action: "For the past 11 years I have, along with my family, worked with, lived among, and advocated for homeless people in the city of Atlanta. When we began our work in 1979, we estimated around 1,500 homeless people in our city. Now there are more than 10,000. This is a direct result of public policy at a local, state, and federal level; it is a direct result of a business community that turns its head and consistently chooses entertainment for the rich over basic life-sustaining resources for the poor. We must take a stand and take it now. The homeless are dying because of our corporate neglect. We must house them now."[394]

Update: Murphy continues to live and serve at the Open Door Community. For many years she has been a member of the Open Door leadership team and the editor of *Hospitality*, where she frequently publishes essays on social justice issues, particularly the death penalty. In 1990, she published *Frances Pauley: Stories of Struggle and Triumph*, an edited collection of stories told by Pauley, a tireless activist for racial and economic justice and a mentor for the Open Door Community. Murphy is currently writing a memoir about living with cancer, tentatively titled *Surely Goodness and Mercy: A Journey into Illness and Solidarity*. Murphy also continues to direct the Southern Prison Ministry, and with her guitar and effervescent voice, she continues to sing for social justice.

Murphy Davis

Elizabeth Dede, 28, is in her fifth year as an advocate with homeless people in Atlanta. A partner at the Open Door Community, Ms. Dede was arrested one year ago for disrupting the opening ceremonies at Underground Atlanta. She connects that previous action with the Imperial Hotel takeover as a continual calling of the city of Atlanta to accountability.

Elizabeth's statement for the Imperial Hotel street action: "A city that spends $142 million on entertainment to develop Underground Atlanta and plans to spend another $1 billion on sports and entertainment for the Olympics must also spend comparable amounts for housing for the homeless and the poor. Vacant and abandoned housing cannot be tolerated when thousands of people have only the streets for their homes. Quoting William Lloyd Garrison, the great abolitionist, 'I am in earnest – I will not equivocate – I will not excuse – I will not retreat a single inch – and I will be heard!' Abolish homelessness now!"

Elizabeth Dede

Update: Elizabeth was a partner at the Open Door Community for many years, where she continued to engage in social justice activism. She later moved to Americus, Georgia, to work with the Prison & Jail Project for six years. She then worked with the Fuller Center for Housing and moved to Koinonia Farm in 2007, where she taught in the home school cooperative with the youngest children of the community. Koinonia Farm is a 70-year-old Christian community that challenges racism, militarism, and materialism. Elizabeth contributes to various media outlets, where she voices challenging perceptions and ideas about race and class issues.

John Flournoy, 51, describes himself as an "angry African American" who has been homeless for five years in the Atlanta area and who is dissatisfied with the attitude toward homelessness in America.

John's statement for the Imperial Hotel street action: "I am dissatisfied with Mayor Maynard Jackson's administration, both present and past, and very disturbed by (former mayor) Andrew Young's administration because they are African Americans but they identify with the power structure rather than their own sisters and brothers."

John Flournoy

Update: John died in 2001 at age 63 in Fitzgerald, Georgia.

Sister Jo Ann Geary, 47, Catholic Sister of St. Joseph of Carondelet, is a Family Nurse Practitioner with Mercy Mobile providing health care to homeless people.

Jo Ann's statement for the Imperial Hotel street action: "Today I stand in solidarity with our homeless sisters and brothers to say, 'Rise up Atlantans and harden not your heart!' It's time, well past time, to stop spending millions of dollars on recreation while thousands in our community go without their basic needs. You can make a difference, you and me and all of us together, can stop this travesty – homelessness."

Update: Currently Jo Ann is in Gulu, Northern Uganda, ministering as a Family Nurse Practitioner in a health center and building a much-needed maternity ward. Prior to this, she worked with migrant farm workers, set up primary care centers in Georgia, ministered in Appalachia, and worked with the Mercy Mobile Health Unit, providing clinics in shelters and church halls during soup kitchens. Immediately following her work with Mercy Mobile and the Imperial Hotel occupation, she went to minister in the Infectious Disease Clinic of Grady Hospital, treating those with HIV/AIDS for ten years.

Sister Jo Ann Geary

Eduard Loring, 50, is a Presbyterian minister and founding partner of the Open Door Community. An advocate for homeless people, Loring has been active among the poor in Atlanta for 15 years.

Eduard's statement for the Imperial Hotel street action: "This action is a Christmas event. We are asking for room in the inn for God's poor in the name of Jesus Christ."

Update: A self-described street theologian, Eduard continues to disrupt business-as-usual in Atlanta. He lives at the Open Door Community, where he maintained a leadership role for over thirty-five years. In addition to raising hell for social justice issues including affordable housing, panhandling ordinances, and the death penalty, Eduard continues to lead prayer, serve meals, and perform works of mercy. He is an associate editor of *Hospitality*, where he frequently contributes essays. Eduard has published three books: *The Cry of the Poor: Cracking White Male Supremacy – An Incendiary and Militant Proposal* (2010); *The Festival of Shelters: A Celebration for Love and Justice* (with Heather Bargeron, 2008); and *I Hear Hope Banging at My Back Door: Writings from Hospitality* (2000).

Eduard Loring

Carol Schlicksup, 44, is a Catholic sister of St. Joseph of Carondelet and a resident volunteer at the Open Door Community for the last ten months.

Carol's statement for the Imperial Hotel street action: "I'm part of this action because I follow Jesus and Jesus is a God of the poor. I'm here to proclaim my rage at the city of Atlanta, her officials, her rich and powerful citizens, her clergy people, her churches and synagogues and social service agencies! I'm here to ask why some of us live in mansions and others live on the streets, to ask why we need so many entertainment centers and ostentatious office buildings rather than buildings to afford permanent shelter to all the citizens

Sister Carol Schlicksup

of this city! I want to know why we spend billions on the new domed stadium, the Olympics, Underground Atlanta, and leave 11,000 people without shelter."

Update: Carol lived at the Open Door for two years as a resident volunteer. During this transitional period in her life, she left her career as a teacher and her calling as a nun. Carol eventually became a licensed psychotherapist, and she practiced marriage and family counseling for over ten years in Memphis, Tennessee. She is currently a practitioner of energy attunement, a holistic healing method that balances the body's energy fields to bring emotional, physical, mental, and spiritual well-being.

C.M. Sherman, 57, is a formerly homeless man who has lived and worked at the Open Door Community for the past two years. He plans to become a partner in that community next month.

C.M.'s statement for the Imperial Hotel street action: "I am a poor black man of 57 who has been pressed to the limits of my tolerance by a city whose policy is 'hurrah for the rich and to hell with the poor.' And because of Atlanta's misdirected priorities resulting in its neglect to provide adequate housing for poverty-stricken people, I was forced to be part of the homeless community for more than 15 years, during which I took residency in the abandoned Imperial Hotel – until they ran the homeless out and sealed

C.M. Sherman

the building. Now, as part of a political action, I have re-entered the building that was once my home to demand justice and housing for the poor."

Update: C.M. led a protest at Woodruff Park after the city had not met its deadline for constructing Welcome House. Later, at the groundbreaking ceremony for Welcome

House, city officials asked C.M. to dig the first shovelful of earth to symbolize progress on its eventual opening. C.M. struggled with alcohol addiction and treatment for many years before finally succumbing to alcohol poisoning on Christmas Eve in the 1990s. He died in the room he rented at Welcome House, a single-room-occupancy hotel that was a direct result of PUJ's occupation of the Imperial Hotel.

Larry Travick, 38, became a resident of the Open Door Community after living on the streets. His background includes a college education at St. Augustine's College and a varied work history. He was homeless when he first came to the Open Door Community in the summer of 1988 for food, a shower, and clothing.

Larry's statement for the Imperial Hotel street action: "After becoming a regular of the soup kitchen and shower line, winter came upon me. With nowhere to stay but the back porch of 910 (the Open Door Community), I was asked to become a member of the community. Since becoming a member of the community, I have been involved in various activities concerning homelessness and urban justice. I am here today involved in this action because I feel that there is a need for justice for the poor and homeless brothers and sisters who don't have a place to call home because our city government feels that it is more important to build domed stadiums and Underground Atlanta than to build homes for the homeless."

Larry Travick

Update: Larry lived for a while at the Open Door after the hotel occupation. He moved out when he began working at First Iconium Baptist Church. He died of complications from AIDS.

Other Notables

Francis Pauley and **Clinton Marsh** were named PUJ honorary co-chairs. Murphy called Francis and Clinton "two great elders." Dr. Marsh was a retired African American Presbyterian minister and, according to Murphy, he was "revered and became more radical the longer he went into retirement." Francis Pauley had previously advised People for Urban Justice, and she was very supportive of the Imperial occupation. In fact, she was at the hotel every afternoon, and became known during this period as Mother PUJ. In her eighties at the time of the occupation, and against her doctor's orders, she sat in a lawn chair in the sweltering heat during the hotel takeover.[395] According to Murphy, she "just loved up on all the homeless folks, and they really loved her." Mother PUJ tee shirts were created in her honor. In 1997, Common Cause Georgia initiated a citizenship award in her name. The first recipient (presented by Pauley) was Bruce Gunter, a leader of Progressive Redevelopment, Inc., the non-profit organization that turned the dilapidated Imperial Hotel into affordable housing in 1996.[396] Pauley died in 2003 at ninety-seven years old.[397]

Rev. Houston Wheeler is a United Church of Christ minister and was an activist organizer with PUJ from 1990 to 1998. Since 1974, Houston has been a community organizer advocating for affordable housing in the arenas of public housing, low-income neighborhoods, and homelessness. In his book *Organizing in the Other Atlanta*, Houston documents how Atlanta's business community for over fifty years has imposed its will and economic power upon city government and low-income neighborhoods, which has caused persistent displacement of poor people.

TIMELINE
HIGHLIGHTS OF THE OCCUPATION

Monday ♦ June 18, 1990

- Eight PUJ members enter the abandoned Imperial Hotel at 4:00 a.m.
- A banner saying "House the Homeless Here!" is unfurled from the top floor of the eight-story building at 11:00 a.m.
- Protesters at street level carry signs supporting PUJ members inside the hotel.
- In the early evening, PUJ sends a letter to building owner John Portman, announcing that the action is no longer symbolic: they will occupy the hotel.
- By nightfall, 50 homeless people join PUJ members inside the hotel.

Tuesday ♦ June 19

- A breakfast of grits, eggs, coffee, and oranges is served to 180 people at the hotel.
- PUJ sends a press release announcing that they have opened the Imperial Hotel to house the poor.

Photo courtesy of the Open Door Community.

- PUJ sends a letter to John Portman asking him to join them and to send a renovation crew.

Wednesday ♦ June 20

- More than 70 homeless people take up residence inside the hotel.
- Occupants clear out rubbish from the hotel, which accumulates in a large pile on the sidewalk.
- Protesters ask city officials to have the trash taken away, but they decline.
- The city orders Portman to clean up the pile of debris. A bulldozer arrives.
- Mayor Maynard Jackson tours the Imperial in the afternoon. He calls it a "dangerous fire trap" and tells occupants that he has asked John Portman to refrain from forcibly removing anyone.
- Occupiers rename the hotel Welcome Home (and later change it to Welcome House).

Photo courtesy of the Open Door Community.

Photo courtesy of the Open Door Community.

Thursday ♦ June 21

- City building inspectors declare the building unsafe.
- Mayor Jackson announces that he is seeking temporary shelter for the occupants.

Friday ♦ June 22

- Aaron Turpeau, chief of staff for Mayor Jackson, offers the Grady High School gym as a temporary shelter.
- Two hundred cots are set up at Grady High, but only six people show up to use them.
- City officials announce that Grady High will be available for three weeks, and that they expect a new shelter to open at 234 Memorial Drive.

Saturday ♦ June 23

- Occupants are now joined by more than 200 people from the street. PUJ member Eduard Loring tells a reporter: "What we wanted to say is that if you are going to spend $142 million for Underground in the '80s, we're going to go above

ground to build housing for the homeless in the '90s."[398]

- Churches, non-profit organizations, and individuals continue to bring food, water, and other necessities to the occupants inside the hotel.
- Mayor Jackson asks Shirley Franklin, executive officer of operations, to take charge of negotiations.
- Shirley Franklin spends a sleepless night in the hotel, meeting privately with homeless occupiers while, apparently, devising a strategy to divide the homeless and homelessness-

Photo by Dwight Ross, Jr. Copyright *Atlanta Journal-Constitution*. Photo courtesy of Georgia State University.

Photo courtesy of the Open Door Community.

activist occupiers inside. After tonight, she visits the hotel every day until negotiations begin.

Sunday ♦ June 24

- Occupants rejuvenate rooms and move up to higher floors as the rooms on the lower floors fill up.
- Signs and banners are placed on the hotel, one of which reads "Homelessness is Not a Crime – An Empty Building Is!"

Wednesday ♦ June 27

- Occupants decline to leave the hotel to march with Rev. Hosea Williams in a rally to urge Nelson Mandela to encourage local leaders to help hungry and homeless people in Atlanta; occupants are wary of city administrators "taking over the takeover" in their absence.

Friday ♦ June 29

- Negotiations are under way between the Executive Committee and city representatives. Housing experts, attorneys, and some PUJ members also attend. By the end of the day,

written proposals from each side are exchanged. Negotiations continue for several days.

Monday ♦ July 2

- Negotiations end around 11:00 p.m., when it is revealed that the Executive Committee agrees to leave the hotel after they are promised, among other items, 3,500 units of affordable housing in the next three and one-half years and immediate jobs at a new, temporary city shelter on Memorial Drive.
- Mayor Jackson and Bill Jones, a member of the Executive

Photo by Dwight Ross, Jr. Copyright *Atlanta Journal-Constitution*. Photo courtesy of Georgia State University.

Committee, hold a press conference in front of the hotel, announcing that a settlement has been reached and the occupation is officially over.

Tuesday ♦ July 3

- Around 7:00 a.m., homeless people inside the hotel begin gathering their belongings in preparation for their bus ride to the city shelter about a mile away.
- By noon, 85 people have been taken by bus to the new shelter, Welcome House.

Image courtesy of the Open Door Community.

- Six of the eight original PUJ members (the "Imperial Eight") who had entered the hotel illegally on Monday, June 18, are on the roof of the hotel's front porch using a bullhorn to broadcast their continuing belief that affordable housing, not temporary shelter, is urgently needed.

SUPPORT THE IMPERIAL HOTEL TAKEOVER

HOMELESSNESS IS NOT A CRIME —AN EMPTY BUILDING IS!!!

Refuse & Resist!

Image courtesy of the Open Door Community.

Photo by Dwight Ross, Jr. Copyright *Atlanta Journal-Constitution*. Photo courtesy of Georgia State University.

- At 12:40 p.m., the six remaining PUJ members at the hotel are arrested and charged with criminal trespass. They are not taken to jail but instead released at the Open Door Community.

AFTERWORD

"HOUSING PRECEDES EQUALITY: THE OCCUPATION OF THE IMPERIAL HOTEL"

A 1991 Reflection by Sister Carol Schlicksup[399]

It was late spring of the year 1990 and the West Hunter Street night shelter, which provided space for 150 to 200 homeless men, had closed for the summer. Some said the shelter would never reopen because neighborhood pressure against it had become so strong. No replacement shelter was provided by the city! Some of our homeless friends had joined us at the Open Door for lunch this day, and they volunteered to lead an effort to bring this problem to the attention of the city. Several of us from the Open Door agreed to join them, and with this decision, a history-making event was born. We developed a petition written to Mayor Maynard Jackson by homeless people demanding that a replacement shelter be opened and proclaiming that housing is a human right! Our friends faithfully came to the Open Door during Sunday breakfasts, daily soup kitchens, and shower lines. They got hundreds of signatures.

We made many an unannounced trip to the mayor's office that spring demanding to see the mayor, "sitting in" until we got some satisfaction. We presented our petition to Aaron Turpeau, the mayor's acting chief of staff. We heard from many different people on the city's payroll; even Maynard Jackson himself walked through one of our meetings on the way to another appointment. Each time we met, we were assured that a building would be located, and a new deadline would be established. I remember one meeting at the Open Door which included shelter directors, Metro Atlanta Task Force for the Homeless staff, and people from the mayor's office. The shelter directors said they'd been looking for a building to use for a shelter for over two years. This process of meetings, phone calls, and broken promises continued for a period of approximately three weeks. Spring wore into summer and no shelter was opened. Our early leadership from homeless people faded, because housing precedes political empowerment and the ability to organize politically. They lost hope! They needed to use their energy to survive.

People for Urban Justice, affectionately known as PUJ, took on the cause. PUJ was born at the Open Door, an outgrowth of attempts to form coalitions across the city to deal with the evils of the labor pool system. PUJ is a political action organization whose members are called to protest violations of human rights in and by the city of Atlanta. Our membership includes people from the Open Door, formerly homeless people, and the medical, legal, church, and advocacy communities in the city. We form a coalition nationally because of our stance against the death penalty. PUJ members chose the date of June 18, 1990, close to the one-year anniversary of the opening of Underground Atlanta, as the time to take action.

The action was to protest the lack of affordable housing in Atlanta, and to oppose the use of billions of dollars for entertainment while 15,000 people were living on the streets. It was a daring plan to occupy an abandoned hotel on the corner of Ralph McGill and Peachtree Streets in downtown Atlanta – the Imperial Hotel. Eight members of People for Urban Justice, some of us formerly homeless people, went into the hotel early on the morning of the eighteenth to unfurl our banner stating "House the Homeless Here!" from the windows on the top floor. Following this we had a demonstration, picketing and leafleting on the street in front of the hotel, and we waited to be arrested and carry our protest to the courts. Arrest didn't come that afternoon, and as we waited on the top floor of the Imperial, I remember wondering how one goes about organizing homeless people. I knew that we needed homeless people to respond to our occupation in order for it to make an impact on our city. Being in the hotel, even with our banner and our bodies hanging out the windows, just didn't seem to matter to anyone. Late that afternoon we opened the doors of the Imperial to homeless people, and through the doors came hope, pain, leadership, and the Spirit of God!

By the evening of June 18 we had some 50 people staying with us. Most evenings after that, between 150 and 300 people stayed at the old Imperial. We put our banners up across the front of the hotel and named our place Welcome House. Well-defined plans were put aside. A shift in leadership took place and People for Urban Justice took on the role of support. Homeless people formed an Executive Committee to lead Welcome House, and community was built. Our purpose was to obtain affordable and decent housing for the poor of Atlanta. We were no longer interested in shelters! Homeless people, often stereotyped as criminals, addicts, and bums, cleaned up the hotel and took responsibility for the decision-making related to maintenance, security, check-in, and distribution of goods. PUJ people became members of the community, kept a presence at the hotel, and participated in and supported decisions made by the Executive Committee. Community meetings and press conferences were held. Even Mayor Jackson, in a history-making event, held a press conference with poor people on the streets of Atlanta. Now, interestingly enough, the city offered a shelter as an alternative to the Imperial. "We want *housing!*" the people shouted.

John Portman, a wealthy Atlanta developer, owned the hotel. We demanded response from him – as well as from the business community – to the plight of the homeless poor in their city. Mr. Portman sent his security personnel to advise us of the dangerous and unsafe conditions in the hotel. The people responded, "The streets are the *most dangerous* place to live!" The people demanded garbage pick-up and portable toilets. After we blocked the street with trash from the hotel and stalled business at Mr. Portman's nearby construction site, we got a dumpster. Eventually, the toilets arrived. However, getting the toilets cleaned and the dumpster emptied was another struggle. We didn't hear from Mr. Portman again, although his lawyer stood at Mayor Jackson's elbow at the press conference and was present at our subsequent arrest.

As our days at Welcome House accumulated, we had visits from many friends and supporters. People brought water, money to run a generator, food, clothes, and themselves to sustain us. People representing the city came too, with a much different purpose. They tried to convince us of the futility and danger of remaining in Welcome House, always offering jobs and shelter. They even sent a van to pick up those who wished to go stay at a high school gym that was opened as a temporary shelter. The people's response was always from the heart, "Shelter is a cuss word around here! We want *housing!*"

Talks began between city officials and Welcome House, represented by the Executive Committee, some members of People for Urban Justice, and experts on housing and the law. There were some 50 homeless people willing to be arrested – with the eight PUJ members who originally occupied the hotel – if our demands weren't met. Negotiations lasted for three days, ending July 2. Our terms were simple: transitional housing for the 150 core members of Welcome House and 5,000 units of affordable single-room-occupancy (SRO) housing to be completed in the three and one-half years left of Mayor Jackson's term. The first 200 units built would house the core members of Welcome House and be managed by the Executive Committee. Affordable housing meant seven dollars a night. The city offered transitional housing in a *shelter* and 3,500 units of SRO housing to be built in the next three and a half years, 1,000 of those units to rent for seven dollars a night. A 17-member advisory committee was to be established: nine members appointed by Welcome House and eight members appointed by the city. Its role would be to monitor the total project and to consult with the mayor as decisions needed to be made.

The biggest stumbling block to the negotiations was our demand for transitional housing. The city didn't want to set a precedent, and additionally couldn't find the $200,000 to pay for hotel rooms to house members of Welcome House until the first SRO was built.[400] Talks wore into the evening, when the members of the Welcome House Executive Committee, who were at the negotiation table, accepted the new shelter on Memorial Drive as a transitional living space. They also accepted jobs managing this new shelter, which they named Welcome House.

People for Urban Justice members, supportive of and understanding the Executive Committee's decision, chose to maintain the integrity of their original purpose: affordable *housing* for *all*. Six PUJ members who entered the Imperial on June 18 chose to be arrested. On the morning of July 3, sixteen days after the occupation of the Imperial Hotel began, and one day before the big Fourth of July parade would have passed by the occupied hotel, city police, with Mr. Portman's lawyer present, charged us with criminal trespass and arrested us. While awaiting our arrest, we stood on the roof of the Imperial and watched as homeless people – members of the Welcome House community – were taken away in buses to the new shelter on Memorial Drive.

Our day in court came about 30 days after we entered the Imperial, and we agreed to plead guilty to the lesser charge of disorderly conduct. Our lawyers, Brian Spears, Michael Hauptman, and Bruce Harvey, were eloquent. Judge Andrew Mickle announced his willingness to suspend our fines if we agreed to use the money to "further our cause" and to never again perform the same action on the Imperial property. Knowing smiles were exchanged as we jubilantly left the courtroom. We'd entered a new arena. The history of advocacy for the poor in the city of Atlanta had been forever changed!

"NO TURNIN' BACK!"

NOTES

PROLOGUE

1. Peter Gathje, e-mail message to author, May 9, 2013.

METHODS

2. Former Atlanta mayor Shirley Franklin (2002-2010), an integral figure in the Imperial Hotel occupation, did not respond to my request for an interview. I do not know if she received my request.

3. J. Todd Moye, *Freedom Flyers: The Tuskegee Airmen of World War II* (New York: Oxford University Press, 2010), 218.

4. Alessandro Portelli, *They Say in Harlan County: An Oral History* (New York: Oxford University Press, 2011), 10.

5. I am drawing from oral historian Valerie Yow's thoughts about historical reconstruction: "By accumulating sources of information and comparing them, we can arrive at an approximate understanding of what happened or is happening and hold this information with some certainty. But there is never absolute certainty about any event, about any fact, no matter what sources are used. No single source or combination of them can ever give a picture of the total complexity of the reality. We cannot reconstruct a past or present event in its entirety because the evidence is always fragmentary." See Yow, *Recording Oral History: A Practical Guide for Social Scientists* (Thousand Oaks, CA: Sage, 1994), 21-22.

INTRODUCTION

6. Charles Steffen, "(Dis)Empowering Homeless People: The Battle for Atlanta's Imperial Hotel, 1990-1991," *Journal of Urban History 38, no. 4* (July 2012): 756, 769, 760, 756.

7. Ibid., 760.

8. Houston Wheeler, interview by author, December 7, 2005. Hereafter, unless cited otherwise, Wheeler's words are from the interview.

9. For a history of the Open Door Community, see Peter R. Gathje, *Christ Comes in The Stranger's Guise: A History of the Open Door Community* (Atlanta: The Open Door Community Press, 1991) and Peter R. Gathje, *Sharing the Bread of Life: Hospitality and Resistance at the Open Door Community* (Atlanta: The Open Door Community Press, 2006). These books are available for free download at http://opendoorcommunity.org/

10. "Hospitality and Resistance in Metro Atlanta." The Open Door Community, accessed July 3, 2014, http://opendoorcommunity.org/

11. Craig Taylor, interview by author, December 23, 2013. Hereafter, unless cited otherwise, Taylor's words are from the interview.

12. Gathje, *Christ Comes in The Stranger's Guise*, 81.

13. Walter Brueggemann, forward to Stanley P. Saunders and Charles L. Campbell's *The Word on the Street: Performing the Scriptures in the Urban Context* (Grand Rapids, MI: William B. Eerdmans Publishing, 2000), xiii.

14. John Sugg, "The 'Atlanta Way' Failed a Generation of Children," Creative Loafing, July 20, 2011. http://clatl.com/atlanta/the-atlanta-way-failed-a-generation-of-children/Content?oid=3620285

15. Atlanta's governing regime and power structure is masterfully portrayed in Tom Wolfe's novel *A Man in Full*, a fictional account of Atlanta's racial and class politics (New York: Bantam Books, 1998).

16. Clarence Stone's words are important here: "It would be an overstatement to suggest that the white business elite has created a black leadership in its own image, but it is no exaggeration that the network of civic cooperation pulls black leadership strongly in that direction." See Stone, *Regime Politics: Governing Atlanta, 1946-1988* (Lawrence: University Press of Kansas, 1989), 194.

17. Ibid., 166.

18. Ronald H. Bayor brings additional insight: "As black politicians assumed control, class divisions over policy became sharply evident in the black community. Class determined which Atlanta blacks would benefit the most. Although both Andrew Young and Maynard Jackson (after his election to a third term in 1989) promised to provide more housing for the poor and to improve their housing stock, very little was done. In the 1980s, when a domed stadium was built in Vine City, the black poor were again displaced, as they would be in the 1990s because of the development needed for the 1996 Olympics." See Bayor, *Race and the Shaping of Twentieth-Century Atlanta* (Chapel Hill: University of North Carolina Press, 1996), 83.

19. Larry Keating, *Atlanta: Race, Class, and Urban Expansion* (Philadelphia: Temple University Press, 2001), 76-77.
20. Stone, *Regime Politics*, 249-50.
21. Houston Wheeler, *Organizing in the Other Atlanta: How the McDaniel-Glenn Leadership Organized to Embarrass and Lead Atlanta's Pharaohs to Produce Affordable Housing in Their Community*, 2nd ed. (Atlanta: Southern Ministry Network, 1998), 31.

CHAPTER ONE: PREPARING FOR STREET ACTION

22. Elizabeth Dede, interview by author, January 15, 2006. Hereafter, unless cited otherwise, Dede's words are from the interview.
23. Walter Brueggemann, *The Prophetic Imagination*, 2nd ed. (Minneapolis: Fortress Press, 2001), 3.
24. Walter Brueggemann, forward to Stanley P. Saunders and Charles L. Campbell's *The Word on the Street: Performing the Scriptures in the Urban Context* (Grand Rapids, MI: William B. Eerdmans Publishing, 2000), xiii. See also Peter R. Gathje's *Christ Comes in The Stranger's Guise* for descriptions and analysis of the spiritual basis of PUJ's street actions.
25. Murphy Davis, interview by author, January 15, 2006. Hereafter, unless cited otherwise, Davis's words are from the interview.
26. Eduard Loring, interview by author, January 15, 2006. Hereafter, unless cited otherwise, Loring's words are from the interview.
27. Information in this paragraph is from David Nordan, "Jackson Convinces Portman to Let Homeless Remain at Site," *Gwinnett Daily News*, June 21, 1990. The statistics for the article were compiled by Bill Holland, statewide coordinator, Metro Atlanta Task Force for the Homeless.
28. Ronald H. Bayor reveals that in 1987 Mayor Andrew Young's administration diverted $6 million in federal funds for the project—money that was designated for Atlanta's low-income populations. See Bayor, *Race and the Shaping of Twentieth-Century Atlanta*, 147.
29. Carol Schlicksup, interview by author, January 13, 2006. Hereafter, unless cited otherwise, Schlicksup's words are from the interview.
30. Similar concerns were voiced in 2013 with the proposed (and later approved) plans for the new Atlanta Falcons stadium that was planned to be built near the old stadium.
31. Jo Ann Geary, interview by author, May 15, 2012. Hereafter, unless cited otherwise, Geary's words are from the interview.
32. Scott Bronstein, "Advocates for Homeless Turn Militant after 'Empty Promises,'" *Atlanta Journal-Constitution*, June 24, 1990.
33. Steffen, "Homeless People," 755.
34. Scott Bronstein, "Advocates for Homeless Turn Militant after 'Empty Promises,'" *Atlanta Journal-Constitution*, June 24, 1990. See also Cynthia Durcanin, "Not in My Neighborhood: SRO Hotels' Reputation Complicates Mayor's Vow," *Atlanta Constitution*, August 3, 1990.
35. Stanley Gibson, interview by author, September 26, 2005. Hereafter, unless cited otherwise, Gibson's words are from the interview.
36. Robert Dobbins, interview by author, November 25, 2005. Hereafter, unless cited otherwise, Dobbins's words are from the interview.
37. Mark Silk, Editorial, "A Promise for the Mayor to Keep," *Atlanta Journal-Constitution*, July 7, 1990.
38. Cynthia Durcanin, "Not in My Neighborhood: SRO Hotels' Reputation Complicates Mayor's Vow," *Atlanta Constitution*, August 3, 1990.
39. Timothy Egan, "In Three Progressive Cities, Stern Homeless Policies," *New York Times*, December 12, 1993; Cynthia Durcanin, "Not in My Neighborhood: SRO Hotels' Reputation Complicates Mayor's Vow," *Atlanta Constitution*, August 3, 1990; Scott Bronstein, "Advocates for Homeless Turn Militant after 'Empty Promises,'" *Atlanta Journal-Constitution*, June 24, 1990.
40. Cynthia Durcanin, "Not in My Neighborhood: SRO Hotels' Reputation Complicates Mayor's Vow," *Atlanta Constitution*, August 3, 1990.
41. Ibid.
42. Lyle V. Harris, "Hotel Set to House TB Patient," *Atlanta Journal-Constitution*, September 30, 1992.
43. Editorial, "Not Enough Room at the Inn," *Atlanta Journal-Constitution*, January 22, 1992.
44. Cynthia Durcanin, "Not in My Neighborhood: SRO Hotels' Reputation Complicates Mayor's Vow," *Atlanta Constitution*, August 3, 1990.
45. Corporation for Supportive Housing, "Supportive Housing Secures Imperial Future for Atlanta's Low Income Community," December 11, 1995.

46. Alma E. Hill, "Many Obstacles to Mayor's Vow to Homeless," *Atlanta Constitution*, July 5, 1990.

47. Ibid.

48. Cynthia Durcanin, "Not in My Neighborhood: SRO Hotels' Reputation Complicates Mayor's Vow," *Atlanta Constitution*, August 3, 1990.

49. Gail Hagans, "City Council Panel to Consider Amendments to Allow SRO Hotels," *Atlanta Journal-Constitution*, June 28, 1990.

50. Some information in this paragraph is from Bruce Gunter's e-mail message to author, August 31, 2013, and from Craig Taylor's interview by author, December 23, 2013.

51. Joe Beasley, interview by author, December 9, 2005.

52. Craig Taylor, interview by author, December 23, 2013.

53. Charles Salter, "Church Says Bank Wary of SRO Plan," *Atlanta Journal-Constitution*, January 9, 1992.

54. Ibid.; Bruce Gunter, e-mail message to author, August 31, 2013. Gunter reported that PRI responded to CAP's concerns about people living with HIV in the area by successfully negotiating for a donated building that housed people living with HIV in a different neighborhood.

55. Lyle V. Harris, "Hotel Set to House TB Patient," *Atlanta Journal-Constitution*, September 30, 1992.

56. Charles Salter, "Church Says Bank Wary of SRO Plan," *Atlanta Journal-Constitution*, January 9, 1992.

57. Editorial, "City Leaders Need a Timeout on Hostel for Working Poor," *Atlanta Journal*, January 14, 1992.

58. Information in this paragraph is from Bruce Gunter's e-mail message to author, August 31, 2013.

59. Ibid.; Craig Taylor, interview by author, December 23, 2013.

60. Lyle V. Harris, "Hotel Set to House TB Patient," *Atlanta Journal-Constitution*, September 30, 1992.

61. "Imperial Hotel," National Park Service, U.S. Department of the Interior, Atlanta: A National Register of Historic Places Travel Itinerary, http://www.nps.gov/nr/travel/atlanta/imp.htm; City of Atlanta, The Imperial Hotel, http://www.atlantaga.gov/index.aspx?page=454

62. Sibley Fleming, "A Promise of New Life," *Atlanta Journal-Constitution*, January 7, 1996.

63. Mara Rose Williams, "Imperial's Majesty Restored," *Atlanta Journal-Constitution*, January 11, 1996; S.A. Reid, "Down-Home Rent for Uptown Living," *Atlanta Journal-Constitution*, December 17, 1996. See the Atlanta Time Machine website for historical photographs and ephemera of some of the nightclubs that were located in the basement of the Imperial Hotel: http://www.atlantatimemachine.com/downtown/imperial.htm See also the History Atlanta website for hotel historical information and photographs: http://historyatlanta.com/the-imperial-hotel/

64. Karen D., interview by author, February 21, 2013. Hereafter, unless cited otherwise, Karen D.'s words are from the interview.

65. Steffen, "Homeless People," 756.

66. Dick Rustay, interview by author, December 5, 2005. Hereafter, unless cited otherwise, Rustay's words are from the interview.

67. "Liberation Theology," British Broadcasting Corporation, last modified July 18, 2011, http://www.bbc.co.uk/religion/religions/christianity/beliefs/liberationtheology.shtml

CHAPTER TWO: BREAKING THE CHAIN

68. Gladys Rustay, interview by author, March 25, 2012. Hereafter, unless cited otherwise, Rustay's words are from the interview.

69. Michael Eric Dyson, *I May Not Get There With You: The True Martin Luther King, Jr.* (New York: Touchstone, 2000), 127-28.

CHAPTER THREE: OPENING THE DOOR

70. Eric Charles White, *Kaironomia: On the Will-to-Invent* (Ithaca: Cornell University Press, 1987), 13.

71. John E. Smith, "Time and Qualitative Time," in *Rhetoric and Kairos: Essays in History, Theory, and Praxis*, eds. Phillip Sipiora and James S. Baumlin (Albany: State University of New York Press, 2002), 55.

72. James H. Cone provides a useful description of liberation theology: "Theology can never be neutral or fail to take sides on issues related to the plight of the oppressed. For this reason it can never engage in conversation about the nature of God without confronting those elements of human existence which threaten anyone's existence as a person. Whatever theology says about God and the world must arise out of its sole reason for existence as a discipline: to assist the oppressed in their liberation. Its language is always language about human liberation, proclaiming the end of bondage and interpreting the religious dimensions of the revolutionary struggle." See Cone, *A Black Theology of Liberation* (Maryknoll, NY: Orbis Books), 4.

73. Frances Fox Piven, *Challenging Authority: How Ordinary People Change America* (Lanham, MD: Rowman and Littlefield, 2006), 23.
74. Ibid., 29.

CHAPTER FOUR: ACTION TO OCCUPATION

75. That afternoon, Murphy and Open Door resident volunteer Amy Yackel toured the building together. Murphy recalled, "I opened the door to a room on the second floor and Amy said 'Murphy, there you are,' and when I looked on the floor there was an old issue of the *Fulton Daily Report* that had a fairly large picture of me that was part of a story on our work on Death Row. The paper was folded over so the picture of me was lying on the floor right inside the door. It was such a weird feeling; it just happened to be there in a pile of trash."
76. People for Urban Justice, letter to John Portman, June 18, 1990.
77. Charles H. Lee, letter to Mayor Andrew Young, November 11, 1989.
78. Ed Loring, "Housing Recognized as Solution to City Homelessness," *Atlanta Journal-Constitution*, March 24, 1990.
79. Stone, *Regime Politics*, 81.
80. Ibid.
81. Ibid.
82. Keating, *Race, Class*, 79.
83. Stone, *Regime Politics*, 95.
84. Ibid., 132.
85. Keating, *Race, Class*, 79.
86. Ibid., 80-81.
87. Stone, *Regime Politics*, 110.
88. Keating, *Race, Class*, 87.
89. Stone, *Regime Politics*, 143.
90. Steffen, "Homeless People," 755.
91. Ibid., 755, 756.
92. This scene recalls the battle for public toilets that the Open Door Community and other concerned groups and residents had been waging since at least 1982. The "Pee for Free with Dignity" campaign encouraged the city to provide public toilets. They reasoned that tourists and residents (including homeless people) would benefit from easy access to clean, plentiful, and free public toilets. See People for Urban Justice, "Chronology of Campaign for Public Toilets," n.d., ca. 1996. This document briefly traces the history of the campaign from 1982 to 1996 (1996 is the assumed date the document was composed, not the end of the campaign).

CHAPTER FIVE: STEADFASTLY UNSETTLED AMONG THE DEBRIS

93. The West Hunter Street Baptist Church was civil rights leader Ralph David Abernathy's congregation.
94. People for Urban Justice, Press Release, June 19, 1990.
95. Ben Smith III, "Protesters Take Over Vacant Historic Property Downtown," *Atlanta Constitution*, June 19, 1990.
96. Ibid.; Ben Smith III, "Activists at Vacant Hotel Say They Won't Leave, Feed 200," *Atlanta Journal*, June 19, 1990.
97. David Nordan, "'Prettiest Room in Town': Breathing New Life Into Old Hotel, Homeless Vow to Continue Vigil," *Gwinnett Daily News*, June 20, 1990.
98. Ibid.
99. Ibid.
100. Jeff Kunerth, "Defiant Check-In at Imperial Hotel: 200 Squatters Find No-Cost Housing," *Orlando Sentinel*, June 24, 1990.
101. David Nordan, "'Prettiest Room in Town': Breathing New Life Into an Old Hotel, Homeless Vow to Continue Vigil," *Gwinnett Daily News*, June 20, 1990.
102. People for Urban Justice, Press Release, June 20, 1990.
103. David Nordan, "Jackson Convinces Portman to Let Homeless Remain at Site," *Gwinnett Daily News*, June 21, 1990.
104. Ibid.
105. Scott Bronstein, "Mayor Calls Old Hotel Dangerous," *Atlanta Constitution*, June 21, 1990.
106. David Nordan, "Jackson Convinces Portman to Let Homeless Remain at Site," *Gwinnett Daily News*, June 21, 1990.

107. Ibid.
108. Ibid.; Pat Murdock, "Mayor Aims to Open Schools as Shelters," *Gwinnett Daily News*, June 22, 1990.
109. Scott Bronstein, "Mayor Calls Old Hotel Dangerous," *Atlanta Constitution*, June 21, 1990.
110. Ibid.
111. Mark Sherman, "Hotel Squatters Snub City's Offer of Shelter," *Atlanta Journal-Constitution*, June 23, 1990.
112. Ibid.
113. Ibid.
114. Jeff Kunerth, "Defiant Check-In at Imperial Hotel: 200 Squatters Find No-Cost Housing," *Orlando Sentinel*, June 24, 1990.
115. Mark Sherman, "Hotel Squatters Snub City's Offer of Shelter," *Atlanta Journal-Constitution*, June 23, 1990; Scott Bronstein, "Advocates for Homeless Turn Militant after 'Empty Promises,'" *Atlanta Journal-Constitution*, June 24, 1990.
116. David Nordan, "Jackson Convinces Portman to Let Homeless Remain at Site," *Gwinnett Daily News*, June 21, 1990; Pat Murdock, "Mayor Aims to Open Schools as Shelters," *Gwinnett Daily News*, June 22, 1990.
117. Loring added that a basic theme in the event is that disciples (Jackson's staff and Portman's attorneys) acted on behalf of their leaders during the occupation.
118. Jeff Kunerth, "Defiant Check-In at Imperial Hotel: 200 Squatters Find No-Cost Housing," *Orlando Sentinel*, June 24, 1990.

CHAPTER SIX: HOSPITALITY IN A BEACON OF BLEAKNESS

119. Scott Bronstein, "Advocates for Homeless Turn Militant after 'Empty Promises,'" *Atlanta Journal-Constitution*, June 24, 1990.
120. Scott Bronstein, "Squatters Discover Sense of Community at 'Our House,'" *Atlanta Journal-Constitution*, June 24, 1990.
121. Scott Bronstein, "Advocates for Homeless Turn Militant after 'Empty Promises,'" *Atlanta Journal-Constitution*, June 24, 1990.
122. "Atlanta: Homeless Take Over Imperial Hotel,' *Revolutionary Worker*, July 8, 1990.
123. John Scruggs, interview by author, November 25, 2005. Hereafter, unless cited otherwise, Scruggs's words are from the interview.

CHAPTER SEVEN: SINGING OUT FOR JUSTICE

124. Ron Eyerman and Andrew Jamison, *Music and Social Movements: Mobilizing Traditions in the Twentieth Century* (Cambridge, UK: Cambridge University Press, 1998), 98.
125. Elise Witt, interview by author, May 21, 2012. Hereafter, unless cited otherwise, Witt's words are from the interview.
126. James West Davidson and Michael Stoff, forward to Allan M. Winkler's *"To Everything There is a Season": Pete Seeger and the Power of Song* (New York: Oxford University Press, 2011), viii-ix.
127. Eyerman and Jamison, *Music and Social Movements*, 163.
128. Ibid.
129. Piven, *Challenging Authority*, 31.
130. Allan M. Winkler, *"To Everything There is a Season": Pete Seeger and the Power of Song* (New York: Oxford University Press, 2011), 40.
131. James West Davidson and Michael Stoff, forward to Winkler's *"To Everything There is a Season,"* ix-x.
132. Eyerman and Jamison, *Music and Social Movements*, 45.
133. Bronstein, "Mayor Calls Old Hotel Dangerous," *Atlanta Constitution*, June 21, 1990.
134. Winkler, *"To Everything There is a Season,"* 99-100.
135. Ibid., 98.
136. Ibid.
137. Eyerman and Jamison, *Music and Social Movements*, 3.
138. Winkler, *"To Everything There is a Season,"* 99.
139. Eyerman and Jamison, *Music and Social Movements*, 66.
140. Ibid., 123.
141. Ibid., 167.
142. Calvin Kimbrough, interview by author, August 16, 2013.
143. David King Dunaway, *How Can I Keep from Singing? The Ballad of Pete Seeger* (New York: Villard Books, 2008), 426.
144. Ibid.

CHAPTER EIGHT: POWER AND UNITY THROUGH SACRIFICE AND STRUGGLE

145. Steffen, "Homeless People," 759.
146. "Atlanta: Homeless Take Over Imperial Hotel," *Revolutionary Worker*, July 8, 1990.
147. Scott Bronstein, "Squatters Won't Leave Imperial to See Mandela," *Atlanta Constitution*, June 27, 1990.
148. "Mandela March for the Homeless," Flyer, n.d.
149. Scott Bronstein, "Squatters Won't Leave Imperial to See Mandela," *Atlanta Constitution*, June 27, 1990.
150. Welcome House Executive Committee, Flyer, n.d.
151. "Atlanta: Homeless Take Over Imperial Hotel," *Revolutionary Worker*, July 8, 1990.

CHAPTER NINE: NEGOTIATIONS AND COLLAPSE

152. Steffen, "Homeless People," 761.
153. Ibid., 761-62.
154. Ibid., 762.
155. Ibid., 763.
156. Ibid., 764.
157. Ibid.
158. Ibid.
159. Ibid.
160. Murphy Davis, Handwritten Notes, People for Urban Justice Files, n.d.
161. Andrew Mickle, interview by author, June 1, 2012. Hereafter, unless cited otherwise, Mickle's words are from the interview.
162. Steffen, "Homeless People," 761.
163. Ibid.
164. Ibid.
165. Piven, *Challenging Authority*, 23.
166. Ibid, 39.
167. Ibid, 31-32.
168. Steffen, "Homeless People," 765.
169. Ibid., 764.
170. Ibid., 758.

CHAPTER TEN: COMPROMISING AND DEFIANT DEPARTURES

171. Mark Sherman and Ben Smith III, "Six Squatters at Old Hotel are Arrested," *Atlanta Journal*, July 3, 1990.
172. Ibid.
173. Pat Murdock, "Homeless Activists Arrested for Refusing to Vacate Hotel," *Gwinnett Daily News*, July 4, 1990.
174. Mark Sherman and Ben Smith III, "Six Squatters at Old Hotel are Arrested," *Atlanta Journal*, July 3, 1990.
175. Ibid.
176. Pat Murdock, "Homeless Activists Arrested for Refusing to Vacate Hotel," *Gwinnett Daily News*, July 4, 1990.
177. Ibid.
178. Mark Sherman, "Mayor Vows Housing for Homeless," *Atlanta Constitution*, July 3, 1990.
179. Mark Sherman, Ben Smith III, "Squatters Find Their Shelter is No Home," *Atlanta Journal-Constitution*, July 4, 1990.
180. Mark Sherman and Ben Smith III, "Six Squatters at Old Hotel are Arrested," *Atlanta Journal*, July 3, 1990.
181. Mark Sherman, Ben Smith III, "Squatters Find Their Shelter is No Home," *Atlanta Journal-Constitution*, July 4, 1990.
182. Ibid.
183. This paragraph is constructed from handwritten People for Urban Justice notes.
184. Schlicksup, "Housing Precedes Equality," 13.
185. Other interviewees suggested that homeless people were also warned that they would be arrested for criminal trespass if they did not depart the building with the Executive Committee.
186. People for Urban Justice, letter to John Portman, July 3, 1990.
187. Pat Murdock, "Homeless Activists Arrested for Refusing to Vacate Hotel," *Gwinnett Daily News*, July 4, 1990.
188. Mark Sherman and Ben Smith III, "Six Squatters at Old Hotel are Arrested," *Atlanta Journal*, July 3, 1990.

189. Schlicksup, "Housing Precedes Equality," 8.
190. Mark Sherman and Ben Smith III, "Six Squatters at Old Hotel are Arrested," *Atlanta Journal*, July 3, 1990.
191. These quotes and some information in this paragraph are from page 13 of Carol Schlicksup's "Housing Precedes Equality." The language used in a newspaper account of the convictions differs from Schlicksup's language. John Blake writes, "Judge Mickle then suspended the fines after they promised not to occupy the place again and donate $75 to a cause of their choice." Based on Blake's account, it does not appear that Judge Mickle was promoting PUJ's efforts to "further" their activism, though it appears that way in Schlicksup's narrative. See Blake's "Housing Activists Convicted," *Atlanta Constitution*, July 19, 1990.
192. John Blake, "Housing Activists Convicted," *Atlanta Constitution*, July 19, 1990.
193. Ibid.

CHAPTER ELEVEN: TOO SLOW WITH THE SROS

194. Eduard Loring, *The Cry of the Poor: Cracking White Male Supremacy—An Incendiary and Militant Proposal* (Atlanta: Open Door Community Press, 2010), 70. Available for free download at: http://opendoorcommunity.org/
195. People for Urban Justice, "City of Atlanta Has Not Kept Its Promise to Homeless Persons," Press Release Packet, March 19, 1991.
196. Frances Pauley, letter to Tom Teepen of *Atlanta Constitution*, March 11, 1991.
197. People for Urban Justice, "We've Waited Nine Long Months!" Flyer, March 19, 1991.
198. People for Urban Justice, "Statement of Purpose: Imperial Action," March 19, 1991.
199. People for Urban Justice, "Nine-Month Anniversary of the Occupation of the Imperial Hotel," Press Release Packet, March 19, 1991.
200. Ibid.
201. People for Urban Justice, "City of Atlanta Has Not Kept Its Promise to Homeless Persons," Press Release, March 19, 1991.
202. Phillip Williams, letter to the editor, *Atlanta Constitution*, April 24, 1991.
203. Houston Wheeler, "For the Sake of the City," *Hospitality* 10, no. 6 (June 1991): 6-7.
204. Ibid., 6.
205. Ibid., 6-7.
206. Ibid., 7.
207. Ibid.
208. Ibid.
209. Ibid.
210. Bruce Gunter, e-mail message to author, August 31, 2013.
211. Mark Sherman, "Hotel Banner Warns Mayor: Don't Forget Housing Vow," *Atlanta Journal-Constitution*, September 13, 1991; Steffen, "Homeless People," 769.
212. Bruce Gunter, e-mail message to author, August 31, 2013.
213. Mark Sherman, "Hotel Banner Warns Mayor: Don't Forget Housing Vow," *Atlanta Journal-Constitution*, September 13, 1991.
214. Ibid.
215. Ibid.
216. Susan Laccetti, "Four Charged in Housing Protest," *Atlanta Journal*, October 24, 1991; Susan Derrick Hinmon and Susan Laccetti, "Advocates for Homeless Interrupt CAP Meeting," *Atlanta Constitution*, October 25, 1991.
217. Susan Laccetti, "Four Charged in Housing Protest," *Atlanta Journal*, October 24, 1991.
218. Ibid.
219. Houston Wheeler, "Thus Saith the Lord of Housing: 'You're Too Slow with the SRO's,'" n.d., ca. late 1991.
220. Ibid.
221. Ibid.
222. Ibid.

CHAPTER 12: WELCOME HOUSE

223. Lyle V. Harris, "A Welcome Wearing Out," *Atlanta Constitution*, August 16, 1990.
224. For details and analysis of these incidents, see Charles Steffen's "Homeless People," 766-68. For newspaper accounts of these incidents, see Lyle V. Harris, "Homeless Shelter Director is Suspended after Arrest,"

Atlanta Constitution, December 18, 1990, and Holly Morris, "City Staff in Charge of Shelter: Two Officers Posted to Deter Incidents," *Atlanta Constitution*, December 19, 1990.

225. Lyle V. Harris, "Homeless Shelter Director is Suspended after Arrest," *Atlanta Constitution*, December 18, 1990.

226. Pat Simms, "Atlanta SRO Project Tests Patience," Federal Reserve Bank of Atlanta, *Partners in Community and Economic Development 3*, no. 2 (Summer 1993): 4.

227. Charles Salter, "$1.4 Million Loan is OK'd for SRO Hotel: Welcome House Will Offer 209 Units for the Homeless," *Atlanta Journal-Constitution*, January 18, 1992.

228. Ibid.

229. Ibid.

230. Ibid.

231. Ibid.

232. John Dunn, "A Heart for the Homeless: Bruce Gunter is Renovating Buildings and Revitalizing Lives," *Georgia Tech Alumni Magazine*, n.d., accessed online September 16, 2005.

233. Lyle V. Harris, "SRO Hotel Gets Mixed Reviews: Homeless Activists Say Truly Needy Aren't Being Served," *Atlanta Journal-Constitution*, December 27, 1992.

234. Pat Simms, "Atlanta SRO Project Tests Patience," 1; Mike Griffin, "From Protest to Partnership: The Story of the Welcome House SRO," Progressive Redevelopment ephemera associated with Welcome House Grand Opening, n.d., ca. December 18, 1992.

235. Pat Simms, "Atlanta SRO Project Tests Patience," 3; Mike Griffin, "From Protest to Partnership: The Story of the Welcome House SRO," Progressive Redevelopment ephemera associated with Welcome House Grand Opening, n.d., ca. December 18, 1992.

236. Pat Simms, "Atlanta SRO Project Tests Patience," 3; Lyle V. Harris, "SRO Hotel Gets Mixed Reviews: Homeless Activists Say Truly Needy Aren't Being Served," *Atlanta Journal-Constitution*, December 27, 1992.

237. Pat Simms, "Atlanta SRO Project Tests Patience," 3, 4.

238. Pat Simms, "Atlanta SRO Project Tests Patience," 4.

239. Mike Griffin, "From Protest to Partnership: The Story of the Welcome House SRO," Progressive Redevelopment ephemera associated with Welcome House Grand Opening, n.d., ca. December 18, 1992.

240. Progressive Redevelopment, "Welcome House: Grand Opening," Program Pamphlet, December 18, 1992.

241. Bruce Gunter, "Imperial Hotel's Rich History Tells Us How We Have Treated Our Poor," *Saporta Report*, December 10, 2010, http://saportareport.com/blog/2010/12/imperial-hotels-rich-history-shows-how-atlanta-has-treated-its-poor/

242. Lyle V. Harris, "SRO Hotel Gets Mixed Reviews: Homeless Activists Say Truly Needy Aren't Being Served," *Atlanta Journal-Constitution*, December 27, 1992; Pat Simms, "Atlanta SRO Project Tests Patience," 12.

243. Progressive Redevelopment, "One Non-Profit's Approach to Affordable Housing," ephemera associated with Welcome House Grand Opening, n.d., ca. December 18, 1992.

244. Corporation for Supportive Housing, "The Basics," http://www.csh.org/supportive-housing-facts/introduction-to-supportive-housing/

245. "A Welcome Site for Working Poor Homeless," *Atlanta Journal-Constitution*, December 19, 1992.

246. Pat Simms, "Atlanta SRO Project Tests Patience," 12.

247. Ibid.

248. Lyle V. Harris, "SRO Hotel Gets Mixed Reviews: Homeless Activists Say Truly Needy Aren't Being Served," *Atlanta Journal-Constitution*, December 27, 1992.

249. Ibid.

250. See Houston Wheeler, "Atlanta's Rejection of Affordable Housing for the Homeless," People for Urban Justice, "A Pre-Olympic Plan for Housing Atlanta's Homeless Persons in Atlanta," n.d., ca. 1993/1994, 14.

251. Lyle V. Harris, "SRO Hotel Gets Mixed Reviews: Homeless Activists Say Truly Needy Aren't Being Served," *Atlanta Journal-Constitution*, December 27, 1992.

CHAPTER THIRTEEN: OLYMPIC DIVERSIONS

252. Emory Thomas Jr., "City Has Olympic Plans but Needs $700 Million," *Atlanta Business Chronicle*, May 15-21, 1992.

253. "Misplaced Priorities: Atlanta, The '96 Olympics, and The Politics of Urban Renewal," n.d., ca. 1991.

254. Ibid.

255. Ibid.

256. Ibid.

257. Ibid.
258. The lyrics and music of this song appear in Houston Wheeler's *Organizing in the Other Atlanta*, 19. The lyrics and music also appear in Murphy Davis's "Olympic Atlanta: Building a House on Sand," *Hospitality* 15, no. 7 (July 1996): 4. This song appears in a slightly different version as "The Homeless Olympics" in Elise Witt's 1993 CD *Mezzanine* (Pine Lake, GA: EMWorld Records).
259. Ed Snodderly, "What Will We Do With the Homeless?" *Southern Changes*, 16, no. 1 (1994), http://beck.library.emory.edu/southernchanges/article.php?id=sc16-1_006
260. Ibid.
261. Metro Atlanta Task Force for the Homeless, "The Criminalization of Poverty: City Ordinances Unfairly Target Homeless People for Arrest," September, 1993, 5. See also "In Better Times," Newsletter, Metro Atlanta Task Force for the Homeless, October/November, 1993, 1-2.
262. Houston Wheeler, "Year End Report – 1992," n.d., ca. December 1992.
263. Ibid.
264. Frances Pauley, letter to Mayor Maynard Jackson, Atlanta City Council President Marvin Arrington, Fulton County Commissioner Michael Lomax, President of Central Atlanta Progress Lewis Holland, and Former President Jimmy Carter, the Atlanta Project, December 1, 1992.
265. Ibid.
266. Ibid.
267. People for Urban Justice, "Atlanta Homeless Manifesto 1993 Agreement," Draft, n.d., ca. December 1, 1992.
268. Houston Wheeler, letter to Mayor Maynard Jackson, Atlanta City Council President Marvin Arrington, Fulton County Commissioner Michael Lomax, President of Central Atlanta Progress Lewis Holland, and Former President Jimmy Carter, representing the Atlanta Project, February 6, 1993.
269. See "The Color of Money: Text of the Pulitzer-Winning Articles" at http://powerreporting.com/color/
270. "Banks Feeling Pressure from Homeless-Advocate Group," *Atlanta Business Chronicle*, September 24-30, 1993.
271. Ibid.
272. Ibid.
273. People for Urban Justice, "Vision of a Beloved Atlanta Community" in "A Pre-Olympic Plan for Housing Atlanta's Homeless Persons in Atlanta," n.d., ca. 1993/1994, 2.
274. Ibid.
275. Houston Wheeler, "Fulfilling the Imperial Hotel Promise," n.d., ca. 1993.
276. People for Urban Justice, "Five-Point Proposal," n.d., ca. October 1993.
277. Sallye Salter, "New Robe for an Old Eyesore: Company Wants to Cover Up the Imperial," *Atlanta Journal-Constitution*, May 13, 1994; Sibley Fleming, "A Promise of New Life," *Atlanta Journal-Constitution*, January 7, 1996; Sallye Salter, "Imperial Hotel to be Renovated as Mixed Housing," *Atlanta Journal-Constitution*, October 28, 1994.
278. Houston Wheeler, letter to Wit B. Carson, III, August 17, 1995.

CHAPTER FOURTEEN: IMPERIAL HOTEL RESURRECTION(S)

279. Bruce Gunter, "Imperial Hotel's Rich History Tells Us How We Have Treated Our Poor," *Saporta Report*, December 10, 2010, http://saportareport.com/blog/2010/12/imperial-hotels-rich-history-shows-how-atlanta-has-treated-its-poor/
280. "Let Rehabilitation Begin," *Atlanta Constitution*, April 10, 1995.
281. Mara Rose Williams, "Imperial's Majesty Restored: Hotel Will Return as Home for Homeless," *Atlanta Journal-Constitution*, January 11, 1996; Charles Steffen, "Sad Lesson in Imperial Hotel's Foreclosure," *Atlanta Journal-Constitution*, November 12, 2010.
282. Bruce Gunter, "Imperial Hotel's Rich History Tells Us How We Have Treated Our Poor," *Saporta Report*, December 10, 2010, http://saportareport.com/blog/2010/12/imperial-hotels-rich-history-shows-how-atlanta-has-treated-its-poor/; Sallye Salter, "$9.5 Million Finally in Place for Renovating Imperial Hotel," *Atlanta Constitution*, October 6, 1995.
283. Bruce Gunter, "Imperial Hotel's Rich History Tells Us How We Have Treated Our Poor," *Saporta Report*, December 10, 2010, http://saportareport.com/blog/2010/12/imperial-hotels-rich-history-shows-how-atlanta-has-treated-its-poor/ Gunter later revealed that his threat of 100 homeless people in the lobby was a ruse: he had no idea how he could do that. Bruce Gunter, e-mail message to author, August 18, 2013.
284. Sallye Salter, "Rebuilding Near for Burned Hotel," *Atlanta Constitution*, March 30, 1995; Cheryl Crabb, "Imperial Hotel is Judged Best Rehabilitation Project," *Atlanta Business Chronicle*, March 7, 1997; Patti

Puckett, "Imperial Hotel Renovations Begin, Despite Funding 'Risk,'" *Atlanta Journal-Constitution*, July 20, 1995; S.A. Reid, "Down-Home Rent for Uptown Living," *Atlanta Journal-Constitution*, December 17, 1996; John Dunn, "A Heart for the Homeless."

285. Cheryl Crabb, "Imperial Hotel is Judged Best Rehabilitation Project," *Atlanta Business Chronicle*, March 7, 1997.

286. Ibid.

287. Mara Rose Williams, "Imperial's Majesty Restored: Hotel Will Return as Home for Homeless," *Atlanta Journal-Constitution*, January 11, 1996.

288. Cheryl Crabb, "Imperial Hotel is Judged Best Rehabilitation Project," *Atlanta Business Chronicle*, March 7, 1997.

289. Mara Rose Williams, "Imperial's Majesty Restored: Hotel Will Return as Home for Homeless," *Atlanta Journal-Constitution*, January 11, 1996.

290. S.A. Reid, "Down-Home Rent for Uptown Living," *Atlanta Journal-Constitution*, December 17, 1996.

291. Corporation for Supportive Housing, "Supportive Housing Secures Imperial Future for Atlanta's Low Income Community," December 11, 1995.

292. Sallye Salter, "$9.5 Million Finally in Place for Renovating Imperial Hotel," *Atlanta Constitution*, October 6, 1995; AFL-CIO Housing Investment Trust, "Imperial Hotel: Project Profile," February 2013, http://www.aflcio-hit.com/user-assets/Documents/project_profiles/Imperial.pdf

293. Bruce Gunter, "Imperial Hotel's Rich History Tells Us How We Have Treated Our Poor," *Saporta Report*, December 10, 2010, http://saportareport.com/blog/2010/12/imperial-hotels-rich-history-shows-how-atlanta-has-treated-its-poor/

294. Progressive Redevelopment, "The Imperial on Peachtree: Grand Opening Ceremony," Program Pamphlet, December 18, 1996; Bruce Gunter, "Imperial Hotel's Rich History Tells Us How We Have Treated Our Poor," *Saporta Report*, December 10, 2010, http://saportareport.com/blog/2010/12/imperial-hotels-rich-history-shows-how-atlanta-has-treated-its-poor/; Yusuf Davis, "Around Town: Play Explores Live Knocked Off Course," *Atlanta Journal-Constitution*, December 19, 1996.

295. Cheryl Crabb, "Imperial Hotel is Judged Best Rehabilitation Project," *Atlanta Business Chronicle*, March 7, 1997.

296. Progressive Redevelopment, "The Imperial on Peachtree: Grand Opening Ceremony," Program Pamphlet, December 18, 1996; AFL-CIO Housing Investment Trust, "Imperial Hotel: Project Profile," February 2013, http://www.aflcio-hit.com/user-assets/Documents/project_profiles/Imperial.pdf

297. Progressive Redevelopment, "The Imperial on Peachtree: Grand Opening Ceremony," Program Pamphlet, December 18, 1996.

298. John Dunn, "A Heart for the Homeless."

299. S.A. Reid, "Down-Home Rent for Uptown Living," *Atlanta Journal-Constitution*, December 17, 1996.

300. Corporation for Supportive Housing, "Imperial Hotel: Fact Sheet," n.d., ca. 1996.

301. John Dunn, "A Heart for the Homeless."

302. S.A. Reid, "Down-Home Rent for Uptown Living," *Atlanta Journal-Constitution*, December 17, 1996.

303. Stacia M. Brown, "A Miracle on Peachtree Street: The Reopening of the Imperial Hotel," *Hospitality* 16, no. 2 (February 1997): 2.

304. Mara Rose Williams, "Imperial's Majesty Restored: Hotel Will Return as Home for Homeless," *Atlanta Journal-Constitution*, January 11, 1996.

305. Ibid.

306. Ibid.

307. S.A. Reid, "Down-Home Rent for Uptown Living," *Atlanta Journal-Constitution*, December 17, 1996.

308. Ibid.

309. Mara Rose Williams, "Imperial's Majesty Restored: Hotel Will Return as Home for Homeless," *Atlanta Journal-Constitution*, January 11, 1996.

310. S.A. Reid, "Down-Home Rent for Uptown Living," *Atlanta Journal-Constitution*, December 17, 1996.

311. John Dunn, "A Heart for the Homeless."

312. Stacia M. Brown, "A Miracle on Peachtree Street," 2.

313. Martha Ezzard, Editorial, "Homeless Part of Imperial's Debut," *Atlanta Journal-Constitution*, November 9, 1996.

314. John Dunn, "A Heart for the Homeless."

315. Ibid.

316. Ibid.

317. Ibid.

318. Bruce Gunter, "Imperial Hotel's Rich History Tells Us How We Have Treated Our Poor," *Saporta Report*, December 10, 2010, http://saportareport.com/blog/2010/12/imperial-hotels-rich-history-shows-how-atlanta-has-treated-its-poor/

319. Cheryl Crabb, "Imperial Hotel is Judged Best Rehabilitation Project," *Atlanta Business Chronicle*, March 7, 1997.

320. Smith Dalia Architects, "Awards: Imperial Hotel," http://www.smithdalia.com/awards/

321. Progressive Redevelopment, "The Imperial SRO: Property-at-a-Glance," Progressive Redevelopment website, 2002-2005, accessed September 16, 2005, information no longer available at the website.

322. Ibid.

323. Bruce Gunter, "Imperial Hotel's Rich History Tells Us How We Have Treated Our Poor," *Saporta Report*, December 10, 2010, http://saportareport.com/blog/2010/12/imperial-hotels-rich-history-shows-how-atlanta-has-treated-its-poor/

324. Maria Saporta, "Historic Imperial Hotel—A Model for Affordable Housing—Now Facing Foreclosure," *Saporta Report*, October 17, 2010, http://saportareport.com/blog/2010/10/historic-imperial-hotel-a-model-for-affordable-housing-now-facing-foreclosure/

325. Ibid.

326. Ibid.

327. Ibid.

328. Ibid.

329. Bruce Gunter, e-mail message to author, August 18, 2013. Gunter also pointed out that operating on such small margins was a structural flaw in the financing.

330. Maria Saporta, "Historic Imperial Hotel—A Model for Affordable Housing—Now Facing Foreclosure," *Saporta Report*, October 17, 2010, http://saportareport.com/blog/2010/10/historic-imperial-hotel-a-model-for-affordable-housing-now-facing-foreclosure/

331. Ibid.

332. Bruce Gunter, "Imperial Hotel's Rich History Tells Us How We Have Treated Our Poor," *Saporta Report*, December 10, 2010, http://saportareport.com/blog/2010/12/imperial-hotels-rich-history-shows-how-atlanta-has-treated-its-poor/

333. Charles Steffen, "Sad Lesson in Imperial Hotel's Foreclosure," *Atlanta Journal-Constitution*, November 12, 2010.

334. Steffen, "Homeless People," 772.

335. PRlog, "Imperial Hotel Purchased by Re-Development Team: Extensive Renovations Will Preserve History," January 17, 2012, http://www.prlog.org/11774673-imperial-hotel-purchased-by-re-development-team-extensive-renovations-will-preserve-history.html

336. National Church Residences, "The Commons at Imperial Hotel Hosts Grand Opening Event March 6th," Recent News, March 6, 2014, http://www.nationalchurchresidences.org/news/recent-news/the-commons-at-imperial-hotel-hosts-grand-opening-event-march-6th; Maria Saporta, "Downtown's Imperial Hotel to be Renovated," *Saporta Report*, January 18, 2012, http://saportareport.com/blog/2012/01/column-downtowns-imperial-hotel-to-be-renovated/ The reduction in the number of units from 120 to 90 was primarily because the new owners deemed that some of the rental units were too small, so they reconfigured space inside the hotel.

337. Maria Saporta, "Downtown's Imperial Hotel to be Renovated," *Saporta Report*, January 18, 2012, http://saportareport.com/blog/2012/01/column-downtowns-imperial-hotel-to-be-renovated/; PRlog, "Imperial Hotel Purchased by Re-Development Team: Extensive Renovations Will Preserve History," January 17, 2012, http://www.prlog.org/11774673-imperial-hotel-purchased-by-re-development-team-extensive-renovations-will-preserve-history.html

338. National Church Residences, "The Commons at Imperial Hotel Hosts Grand Opening Event March 6th," Recent News, March 6, 2014, http://www.nationalchurchresidences.org/news/recent-news/the-commons-at-imperial-hotel-hosts-grand-opening-event-march-6th

339. Carol L. Pearson et al., "The Applicability of Housing First Models to Homeless Persons with Serious Mental Illness: Final Report," U.S. Department of Housing and Urban Development, July 2007, 2, http://www.huduser.org/portal/publications/hsgfirst.pdf

340. National Church Residences, "The Commons at Imperial Hotel Hosts Grand Opening Event March 6th," Recent News, March 6, 2014, http://www.nationalchurchresidences.org/news/recent-news/the-commons-at-imperial-hotel-hosts-grand-opening-event-march-6th; PRlog, "Imperial Hotel Purchased by Re-Development Team: Extensive Renovations Will Preserve History," January 17, 2012,

http://www.prlog.org/11774673-imperial-hotel-purchased-by-re-development-team-extensive-renovations-will-preserve-history.html

341. National Church Residences, "The Commons at Imperial Hotel Hosts Grand Opening Event March 6th," Recent News, March 6, 2014, http://www.nationalchurchresidences.org/news/recent-news/the-commons-at-imperial-hotel-hosts-grand-opening-event-march-6th

342. The Enterprise Foundation, "MetLife Foundation 2000 Awards for Excellence in Affordable Housing: Progressive Redevelopment, Inc., Welcome House SRO Apartments," Metropolitan Life Foundation Awards for Excellence in Affordable Housing, 2001, http://www.knowledgeplex.org/showdoc.html?id=163362

343. Stephen K. Cooper, "Atlanta Project for Homeless Enhanced, Preserved through Resyndication," *Tax Credit Advisor*, May 2009.

344. Ibid.

345. Action Ministries, "Action Ministries and Project Interconnections Celebrate Grand Reopening of Atlanta's Welcome House," Press Release, February 14, 2013.

346. Bruce Gunter, e-mail message to author, August 31, 2013.

CHAPTER FIFTEEN: REFLECTIONS ON SUCCESS

347. Saunders and Campbell, *Word on the Street*. 9.

348. Loring, *Cry of the Poor*, 29.

349. Ibid., 33.

350. Rustay's thoughts about the diminishing compassion for homeless people are mirrored in Timothy Egan's "In Three Progressive Cities, It's Law vs. Street People," *New York Times*, December 12, 1993, and in Lynette Lamb's "Compassion Fatigue: Faced Constantly with Outstretched Hands, Have Americans Hardened Their Hearts?" *Utne Reader*, July/August, 1992.

351. Peter Maurin, co-founder of the Catholic Worker Movement with Dorothy Day in 1933, said: "If the Catholic Church is not today the dominant social dynamic force, it is because Catholic scholars have taken the dynamite of the Church. Catholic scholars have taken the dynamite of the Church, have wrapped it up in nice phraseology, placed it in an hermetic container, and sat on the lid. It is about time to blow the lid off so the Catholic Church may again become the dominant social dynamic force." See Marc H. Ellis, *Peter Maurin: Prophet in the Twentieth Century* (Washington, DC: Rose Hill Books, 1981), 47.

CHAPTER SIXTEEN: OPEN DOOR ACTIVISM

352. Saunders and Campbell, *Word on the Street*, 11.

353. Loring, *Cry of the Poor*, 82.

354. Saunders and Campbell, *Word on the Street*, 77-78.

355. Stone, *Regime Politics*, 169, 174.

356. Ibid., 133.

357. Ibid., 97.

358. Ibid., 97.

359. Ibid., 194.

360. Ibid., 165.

361. Ibid., 208.

362. Saunders and Campbell, *Word on the Street*, 14-15.

363. Loring, *Cry of the Poor*, 54.

364. Saunders and Campbell, *Word on the Street*, 158-159.

365. Loring acknowledges this in *The Cry of the Poor*: "By the political structures, cultural values and religious practices of my nation, I accrue benefits from my patriarchal and racist society every time I step among the 170 disinherited people, hungry and exhausted at 5 a.m., in my front yard on Ponce de Leon Avenue" (18).

366. Loring, *Cry of the Poor*, 42.

367. Ibid., 70-71.

368. Ibid., 70.

CHAPTER SEVENTEEN: KEEP ON KEEPING ON AT THE OPEN DOOR

369. Frances Fox Piven and Richard A. Cloward, *Poor People's Movements: Why They Succeed, How They Fail* (New York: Vintage Books, 1979), 12.

370. Piven and Cloward, *Poor People's Movements*, 3-4.

371. Piven, *Challenging Authority*, 139.

372. Ibid.
373. Ibid.
374. Walter Brueggemann, forward to *TheWord on the Street*, by Stanley P. Saunders and Charles L. Campbell, xiv.
375. Piven and Cloward, *Poor People's Movements*, 1.
376. Ibid., 6.
377. Piven and Cloward, introduction to *Poor People's Movements*, xxi.
378. Ibid.
379. Ibid., xxii.
380. Loring, *Cry of the Poor*, 70.
381. Piven and Cloward, introduction to *Poor People's Movements*, xiii.
382. Ibid.
383. Piven and Cloward, *Poor People's Movements*, 7.
384. Frances Fox Piven and Richard A. Cloward, *Regulating the Poor:The Functions of PublicWelfare* (New York: Pantheon Books, 1971), 338.
385. Piven and Cloward, *Poor People's Movements,* 7.
386. Ibid.
387. Ibid.
388. Loring, *Cry of the Poor*, 70.
389. Ibid., 79.

EPILOGUE

390. Cynthia Tucker, "There's No Simple Answers to City's Homeless Problem," *Atlanta Journal-Constitution*, July 7, 1990.
391. Taylor also pointed out that prior to the hotel occupation he and others were meeting monthly at the Atlanta Community Food Bank to discuss SRO housing development. He recalled that they focused on three particular housing issues: cost per day, number of units, and location.
392. Murphy Davis, "Imperial Surprises," Handwritten Notes, People for Urban Justice Files, n.d.
393. Stacia M. Brown, "A Miracle on Peachtree Street," 2.

"IMPERIAL EIGHT" BIOGRAPHIES

394. Davis's and others' statements in this section are from "People for Urban Justice Press Packet," June 18, 1990.
395. Richard L. Eldredge, "Pauley's Tenacity Rewarded," *Atlanta Journal-Constitution*, February 25, 1997.
396. Ibid.
397. For more details about Pauley's activism, see *Frances Pauley: Stories of Struggle and Triumph*, ed. Murphy Davis (Atlanta: The Open Door Community Press, 1996). This book is available for free download at http://opendoorcommunity.org/

TIMELINE

398. Jeff Kunerth, "Defiant Check-In at Imperial Hotel: 200 Squatters Find No-Cost Housing," *Orlando Sentinel*, June 24, 1990.

AFTERWORD

399. This section uses Carol Schlicksup's 1991 essay, "Housing Precedes Equality: The Occupation of the Imperial Hotel," to provide readers a sense of the political and historical context in which the Imperial Hotel occupation took place. This version of Schlicksup's essay has been edited, so it differs slightly from the original. See *Hospitality* 10, no. 1 (January 1991): 8-13.
400. Barbara Segal astutely points out that it is unclear if Schlicksup means a precedent for providing housing, negotiating with activists, or listening to the public. In a December 17, 2013, telephone interview with the author, Schlicksup reported that, after reviewing her words twenty years after the event, the overall context of her words and her memory suggest that the city did not want to set precedent by providing housing and negotiating with activists.

BIBLIOGRAPHY

Interviews

Joe Beasley, Interview by author. Atlanta, Georgia, December 9, 2005.

Murphy Davis, Interview by author. Atlanta, Georgia, January 15, 2006.

Elizabeth Dede, Interview by author. Atlanta, Georgia, January 15, 2006.

Robert Dobbins, Interview by author. Atlanta, Georgia, November 25, 2005.

Karen D., Interview by author. Oakwood, Georgia, February 21, 2013.

Jo Ann Geary, Telephone interview by author. May 15, 2012.

Stanley Gibson, Interview by author. Atlanta, Georgia, September 26, 2005.

Calvin Kimbrough, Interview by author. Atlanta, Georgia, August 16, 2013.

Eduard Loring, Interview by author. Atlanta, Georgia, January 15, 2006.

Andrew Mickle, Interview by author. Atlanta, Georgia, June 1, 2012.

Dick Rustay, Interview by author. Atlanta, Georgia, December 5, 2005.

Gladys Rustay, Interview by author. Atlanta, Georgia, March 25, 2012.

Carol Schlicksup, Telephone interview by author. January 13, 2006.

John Scruggs, Interview by author. Atlanta, Georgia, November 25, 2005.

Craig Taylor, Telephone interview by author. December 23, 2013.

Houston Wheeler, Interview by author. Atlanta, Georgia, December 7, 2005.

Elise Witt, Telephone interview by author. May 21, 2012.

Newspapers

Atlanta Business Chronicle
Atlanta Journal
Atlanta Constitution
Atlanta Journal-Constitution
Creative Loafing
Gwinnett Daily News
Hospitality
New York Times
Orlando Sentinel
Revolutionary Worker

Books

Bayor, Ronald H. *Race and the Shaping of Twentieth-Century Atlanta*. Chapel Hill: University of North Carolina Press, 1996.

Brueggemann, Walter. *The Prophetic Imagination*. 2nd ed. Minneapolis: Fortress Press, 2001.

Cone, James H. *A Black Theology of Liberation*. 1986. Maryknoll, NY: Orbis Books, 2010.

Dunaway, David King. *How Can I Keep from Singing? The Ballad of Pete Seeger*. New York: Villard Books, 2008.

Dyson, Michael Eric. *I May Not Get There With You: The True Martin Luther King, Jr*. New York: Touchstone, 2000.

Ellis, Marc H. *Peter Maurin: Prophet in the Twentieth Century*. Washington, DC: Rose Hill Books, 1981.

Eyerman, Ron, and Andrew Jamison. *Music and Social Movements: Mobilizing Traditions in the Twentieth Century*. Cambridge, UK: Cambridge University Press, 1998.

Gathje, Peter R. *Christ Comes in The Stranger's Guise: A History of the Open Door Community*. Atlanta: The Open Door Community Press, 1991. Print. Available for free download at the Open Door Community website: http://opendoorcommunity.org/

------. *Sharing the Bread of Life: Hospitality and Resistance at the Open Door Community*. Atlanta: The Open Door Community Press, 2006. Print. Available for free download at the Open Door Community website: http://opendoorcommunity.org/

Keating, Larry. *Atlanta: Race, Class, and Urban Expansion*. Philadelphia: Temple University Press, 2001.

Loring, Eduard. *The Cry of the Poor: Cracking White Male Supremacy— An Incendiary and Militant Proposal*. Atlanta: Open Door Community Press, 2010. Print. Available for free download at the Open Door Community website: http://opendoorcommunity.org/

Moye, J. Todd. *Freedom Flyers: The Tuskegee Airmen of World War II*. New York: Oxford University Press, 2010.

Piven, Frances Fox. *Challenging Authority: How Ordinary People Change America*. Lanham, MD: Rowman and Littlefield, 2006.

Piven, Frances Fox, and Richard A. Cloward, *Poor People's Movements: Why They Succeed, How They Fail*. New York: Vintage Books, 1979.

------. *Regulating the Poor: The Functions of Public Welfare*. New York: Pantheon Books, 1971.

Portelli, Alessandro. *They Say in Harlan County: An Oral History.* New York: Oxford University Press, 2011.

Saunders, Stanley P., and Charles L. Campbell. *The Word on the Street: Performing the Scriptures in the Urban Context.* Grand Rapids, MI: William B. Eerdmans Publishing, 2000.

Smith, John E. "Time and Qualitative Time." In *Rhetoric and Kairos: Essays in History, Theory, and Praxis*, edited by Phillip Sipiora and James S. Baumlin, 46-57, Albany: State University of New York Press, 2002.

Stone, Clarence. *Regime Politics: Governing Atlanta, 1946-1988.* Lawrence: University Press Kansas, 1989.

Wheeler, Houston. *Organizing in the Other Atlanta: How the McDaniel-Glenn Leadership Organized to Embarrass and Lead Atlanta's Pharaohs to Produce Affordable Housing in Their Community.* 2nd ed. Atlanta: Southern Ministry Network, 1998.

White, Eric Charles. *Kaironomia: On the Will-to-Invent.* Ithaca: Cornell University Press, 1987.

Winkler, Allan M. *"To Everything There is a Season": Pete Seeger and the Power of Song.* New York: Oxford University Press, 2011.

Yow, Valerie. *Recording Oral History: A Practical Guide for Social Scientists.* Thousand Oaks, CA: Sage, 1994.

Essays and Reports

Brown, Stacia M. "A Miracle on Peachtree Street: The Reopening of the Imperial Hotel." *Hospitality* 16, no. 2 (February 1997): 1-2.

Dunn, John. "A Heart for the Homeless: Bruce Gunter is Renovating Buildings and Revitalizing Lives." *Georgia Tech Alumni Magazine*, n.d.

Metro Atlanta Task Force for the Homeless. "The Criminalization of Poverty: City Ordinances Unfairly Target Homeless People for Arrest." September, 1993.

"Misplaced Priorities: Atlanta, The '96 Olympics, and the Politics of Urban Renewal." n.d., ca. 1991.

Pearson, Carol L., Gretchen Locke, Ann Elizabeth Montgomery, and Larry Buron. "The Applicability of Housing First Models to Homeless Persons with Serious Mental Illness: Final Report." U.S. Department of Housing and Urban Development, July 2007. http://www.huduser.org/portal/publications/hsgfirst.pdf

Schlicksup, Carol. "Housing Precedes Equality: The Occupation of the Imperial Hotel." *Hospitality* 10, no. 1 (January 1991): 8-13.

Simms, Pat. "Atlanta SRO Project Tests Patience," Federal Reserve Bank of
Atlanta, *Partners in Community and Economic Development* 3, no. 2
(Summer 1993): 1-12.

Snodderly, Ed. "What Will We Do With the Homeless?" *Southern Changes* 16,
no. 1 (1994): 14-15. http://beck.library.emory.edu/southernchanges/
article.php?id=sc16-1_006

Steffen, Charles G. "(Dis)Empowering Homeless People: The Battle for
Atlanta's Imperial Hotel, 1990-1991." *Journal of Urban History* 38, no. 4
(July 2012): 753-776. Education Research Complete, EBSCOhost
(accessed June 27, 2014).

Wheeler, Houston. "For the Sake of the City." *Hospitality* 10, no. 6
(June 1991): 6-7.

ACKNOWLEDGEMENTS

Eduard Loring has been extraordinarily patient. He first approached me about writing the history of the Imperial Hotel occupation from the perspective of the Open Door Community in 2005. When I began the project I was a regular, active volunteer at the Open Door's Monday Morning Breakfast. I was connected. Various things took me away from that regularity and from keeping a rigorous, steady pace with the book: completing a doctoral dissertation; beginning a full-time job; grieving the deaths of my parents, Roberta and Gary, and my brother, Mike; and welcoming the birth of my son, Theodore. During this time Eduard has been wonderfully supportive, and I thank him for his loving patience. I also thank him for his trust and encouragement.

When I began listening to people's passionate accounts of the hotel occupation and reading documents associated with it, I discovered the intense drama that imbued the events. In the pages that follow, I have tried to capture that drama and intensity. Special thanks to Eduard Loring and Houston Wheeler for opening their files to me. These documents allowed me to tell a far richer story.

I have had the generous support of three skillful and articulate editors: Barbara Segal, Jessica Sully, and Heather Bargeron. Their keen attention to clarity, content, and cohesiveness helped shape the narrative from the minutest of details to the largest of the thematic elements. This book would have suffered tremendously without their assistance. Special thanks to the Open Door Community for allowing them to be available to read drafts and assist in myriad other ways. Barbara Segal deserves a special thank you for volunteering her time to do the layout and design as she transformed the plain manuscript into a visually appealing book.

As the copy editor, Julie Martin used her deft editing and communication skills to shepherd the manuscript draft into a book. Mary Catherine Johnson was an excellent liaison in the final stages of production.

I would also like to thank readers who reviewed all or parts of this book: Murphy Davis, Peter Gathje, Bruce Gunter, Eduard Loring, David Mann, and Houston Wheeler. Their astute comments and probing questions made this a better book. If any factual errors or writing blunders remain, they are my own.

In addition to being an invaluable sounding board for oral history research in general, Daniel Kerr's comments about this project helped me think more clearly about the occupation's potential for positively affecting people's lives.

The School of Humanities and Fine Arts at Gainesville State College (now College of Arts and Letters at University of North Georgia) provided financial assistance that enabled me to present draft sections of the book manuscript at academic conferences, where I received valuable feedback.

My sincere gratitude to the people who offered their time and generosity in oral history interviews: Joe Beasley, Murphy Davis, Elizabeth Dede, Robert Dobbins, Karen D., Jo Ann Geary, Stanley Gibson, Calvin Kimbrough, Eduard Loring, Andrew Mickle, Dick Rustay, Gladys Rustay, Carol Schlicksup, John Scruggs, Craig Taylor, Houston Wheeler, and Elise Witt. Without their memories, this book would be far less rewarding for readers.

Finally, thanks to all the housed and un-housed people who summoned the courage to take part in the occupation in ways large and small. Even though they remain largely invisible and without voice in the historical record, their efforts to promote social justice deserve merit and gratitude. Eduard Loring's poetic imagination is evocative when he observes that despite activists' continuing efforts to create additional affordable housing, "Homeless people still roam Atlanta's streets, abandoned as an empty hotel on a moonless night."

Through all of the years I worked on this project my constant companion, Theresa Same, has been enthusiastic and loyal. Her support in all aspects of our life together has never wavered, despite my frequent actions that gave her reason to do so.

Thank you for reading this book!

If you are seeking ways to build the Beloved Community . . .

Come and visit us for a day, a week, or a month.
Join us as a Resident Volunteer.
Lend us a hand as we serve our friends from
the streets and in prison.
We need men's clothes, shoes, food, money, prayer,
blankets and daily volunteers.

Let us hear from you. We can be reached at:

The Open Door Community
910 Ponce de Leon Avenue N.E.
Atlanta, GA 30306-4212
(404) 874-9652
opendoorcommunity.org

Other publications from the Open Door Community

The Cry of the Poor: Cracking White Male Supremacy – An Incendiary and Militant Proposal, by Eduard Loring (2010)

The Festival of Shelters: A Celebration for Love and Justice, by Eduard Loring with Heather Bargeron (2008)

Sharing the Bread of Life: Hospitality and Resistance at the Open Door Community, by Peter R. Gathje (2006)

A Work of Hospitality: The Open Door Reader 1982–2002, edited by Peter R. Gathje (2002)

I Hear Hope Banging at My Back Door: Writings from Hospitality, by Eduard Loring (2000)

Christ Comes in the Stranger's Guise: A History of the Open Door Community, by Peter R. Gathje (1991)

Frances Pauley: Stories of Struggle and Triumph, edited by Murphy Davis (1990)

All of these titles can be ordered from the
Open Door Community or downloaded from our website:
opendoorcommunity.org/resources/publications